How My Addiction Saved My Life

Tashonda Bryant

Dedication

In profound reverence and admiration, I dedicate this book to my beloved mother, Patricia Ann Foust.

You have been a pillar of strength and an unwavering source of love and support. Your boundless encouragement and belief in my abilities have driven my pursuit of writing this book. Your nurturing guidance and the values you instilled in me have shaped the person I am and the words I pen on these pages.

You have been a constant source of inspiration, teaching me the importance of perseverance and determination. Your unwavering faith in my dreams has been a beacon of light during the darkest moments of this creative journey. Your love has been a wellspring of comfort, lifting me during times of doubt.

As I present this work to the world, I am humbled and grateful for the countless sacrifices you have made for me. Your belief in my potential has given me the courage to share my thoughts and ideas, hoping they may touch the lives of others just as you have touched mine.

This book is a tribute to your immeasurable love and your profound impact on my life. I am eternally

Acknowledgment

I would like to extend my heartfelt gratitude to the Almighty for His unwavering support and guidance throughout the journey of writing this book. His presence and belief in me have been a constant source of strength and inspiration.

I am profoundly grateful to my husband, Robert, whose love, encouragement, and unwavering belief in my abilities have made this book a reality. His steadfast support and understanding have been invaluable.

My heartfelt appreciation goes to my daughter, Maya, whose unwavering faith in me and continuous prayers have motivated me during challenging times. Her belief in my endeavors has been a driving force behind this work.

I would also like to thank my son, Robert, whose determined efforts to support his mother deeply touched my heart. His love and actions have strengthened my resolve to create something meaningful and inspiring for others.

Lastly, I thank all the individuals who have offered support, encouragement, and valuable insights while writing this book. Your contributions have played a vital role in shaping and making this work possible.

Thank you all for being a part of this journey and for your firm belief in me. Your support has made a profound difference, and I hope this book will touch the lives of many and inspire others.

Contents

Dedication iii

Acknowledgment v

About the Author ix

Chapter 1 1

Chapter 2 8

Chapter 3 12

Chapter 4 19

Chapter 5 26

Chapter 6 35

Chapter 7 43

Chapter 8 51

Chapter 9 60

Chapter 10 68

Chapter 11 79

Chapter 12 92

Chapter 13 106

Chapter 14 122

Chapter 15 126

Chapter 16 133

Chapter 17 137

Chapter 18 142

Chapter 19 145

Chapter 20 149

Chapter 21 153

Chapter 22 156

Chapter 23 162

Chapter 24 167

Chapter 25 173

Chapter 26 176

Chapter 27 179

Chapter 28 182

Chapter 29 185

Chapter 30 188

Epilogue 191

Chronicles of Denise 193

About the Author

Tashonda Bryant, a resilient individual hailing from the vibrant streets of South Philadelphia, emerged as a beacon of strength and determination in the face of life's adversities. Born to Patricia Ann Foust as the only child, Tashonda's upbringing was marked by the challenges that molded her into the tenacious person she is today.

Despite facing life's struggles and pains, Tashonda's unwavering drive was fueled by the trials that sought to hinder her progress. Her journey through these hardships shaped her character and instilled in her a unique resilience that set her apart.

Tashonda's pursuit of education became a testament to her perseverance, culminating in her graduation from High School and attaining a degree in Pharmacy Technician. This academic achievement symbolized her intellectual prowess and demonstrated her commitment to personal growth and excellence.

Fueled by deep love and passion for helping others, Tashonda embarked on a remarkable entrepreneurial journey. Her soap business, born out of a desire to make a positive impact, became a platform through which she extended assistance to hundreds of young and old individuals grappling with various skin imperfections. Through her products, Tashonda offered tangible solutions and became a source of inspiration for those facing similar challenges.

The underlying theme of love and faith in Tashonda's life narrative is a testament to her enduring spirit. Her unshakable trust in God's plan became the guiding force that propelled her forward, shaping her into an individual whose story is not just about overcoming obstacles but about transforming adversity into opportunities for growth and empowerment.

In essence, Tashonda Bryant's life is a testament to the power of resilience, education, compassion, and faith—a narrative that inspires others to embrace their journeys with hope, determination, and an unwavering belief in the beauty of God's plan.

Chapter 1

"The greater a child's terror, and the earlier it is experienced, the harder it becomes to develop a strong and healthy sense of self."

— *Nathaniel Branden,*
Six Pillars of Self-Esteem

Childhood forms the basis of the person you will become later. It's the base of the vase of your life being shaped on a potter's wheel; if the base goes wrong, it is extremely difficult to shape the rest of the vase in a way that allows it to find balance and not tip over and fall every time there is a slight momentum.

Most people have nothing but warm, fond memories of their childhood. For them, the word 'childhood' is a throwback to simpler times when you could afford to see the world through rose-tinted lenses. When you woke up early in the morning before most of the adults in the house did and watched television in the living room as your mother made pancakes for breakfast. When falling was more likely to mean stumbling onto the dirt face-first while playing, and even if you scraped your knees and cried for a while, there was always the surety that you could get up, rid your hands of the dust from the ground, and then eventually start playing again.

But some of us are not as fortunate as the rest. Since they came into this world and opened their eyes, they were well aware of the harsh realities of life. Misery was a house guest who had overstayed to the point it was now a resident of the house, and his clothes might catch on the sharp edges of the broken house windows and doors, but it did not matter how they did it, as long as they managed to escape.

While it should have been easier to heal, away from the root of it all, sometimes you land, escaping from one toxic sludge right into another. When it happens quite a few times in a row, you might find yourself in a position where you are too tired to even want to fight for your salvation anymore.

My life was something like this, too. As a child, I used to live with my aunt, whom we will call Bertha. My introduction to the difficulties of life started from her treatment of me, which was, to say the least, downright horrendous and something that I hope no other child has to go through ever again. Aunt Bertha was an abusive woman — emotionally and physically. She would mistreat me on a daily basis and abuse me very often, beating me to the point where it got hard to even move around after a beating.

As a child who had never understood love — for you need to be loved to be able to understand what it truly is — I would gloss over those beatings in my head and tell myself that it was all only out of love and concern because that's what most parents tell their kids, isn't it? Now that I know what it really means to be loved and cared for, and now that I have experienced relationships where I was not abused or gaslighted, all I ever see when I look back on my childhood is an older woman who had no other way of letting her frustrations out. So she made use of a mere kid as a punching bag, unconcerned with the kind of scars such trauma leaves on a person.

I was not allowed to make any friends, for all the chores I would be assigned by my aunt did not leave much time for mingling with other kids my age. If I had

had friends, maybe it would have made my life more bearable back then. But despite all that, I did have one friend — Nana.

I met Nana on a day when I got a beating from my aunt for burning some food because she was in a particularly foul mood, even though she was the one who had put it on the stove. I paid the price when I reminded her that she had not, in fact, asked me to keep an eye on the food, and as such, I did not know if something was being cooked.

By then, I had learned to simply deal with the pain — both emotional and abusive. Most days, I managed to keep my tears in check, which was good for me because if there was something my aunt hated more than me, it was my crying, which I understood from the extended abuse I had to deal with when I shed tears after a beating.

That day was particularly bad. My entire body ached, and all my bones were screaming in agony — it felt like something akin to being set on fire. I made it to my room without a single sob, but it was when I lowered my body onto the mattress and it stung to lie down; the dam broke, and I burst into tears, sobbing into the pillow, trying to muffle the sound.

Suddenly, I heard a voice coming from the wall. It sounded like a girl my age, saying comforting things and trying to get me to stop crying. Sniffling, I got up from the bed and limped over; I laid down with my back next to the cold wall and fell asleep to the peaceful lull of her voice.

Gradually, Nana and I became best friends. There was nothing Nana did not know about me, and there were no secrets between the two of us. Everything that went on in my life, Nana knew all about it — the conversations I overheard, things Aunt Bertha said to me, my thoughts and ideas, and opinions. She became my safe haven; the entire day, I could not wait for nightfall each day to be able to retreat to my room and converse with my best friend, entrusting her with my secrets and getting weight off my chest by ranting about my day to her.

It was in August 1992 that I began high school, which is where my previously stagnant story begins. I was not very happy with the fact that I had to leave my family behind to go to school and the fact that I was a city girl through and through, so it was unusual for me to live in the countryside.

My attitude towards living in the country was like mixing oil and water together — they simply don't belong together. I suppose you could say it was beautiful if you were a nature-loving person. There were fields of cotton, something that I had never seen before in my life, and since it was the harvest season, there were men and women picking cotton balls everywhere, as far as the eye could see. Me? All I could think about was going back to my own home — this was clearly not a place where I belonged.

The people that I met there initially were not my type either. There were mostly farmer's kids, and at first, I was skeptical about making any friends at all. But later, I started meeting the more sophisticated crowd, people who were more my type: kids from New Jersey and New York and the like, you get the gist. I started to feel more comfortable and felt like I fit in.

It was then that I met Mike.

Mike was from New York, and his father was a pastor who owned one of the biggest churches. He had the kind of magnetic attitude that you can find only in a New Yorker, the kind that dominates a whole room with its presence. It was nice that he was no eye sore either — quite the contrary, actually. Mike and I became great friends in no time, always hanging out and spending time together.

Chapter 2

"Falling in love is very real, but I used to shake my head when people talked about soul mates, poor deluded individuals grasping at some supernatural ideal not intended for mortals but sounded pretty in a poetry book. Then, we met, and everything changed; the cynic has become the converted, the skeptic, an ardent zealot."

— E.A. Bucchianeri, Brushstrokes of a Gadfly

Leaving familiar surroundings and people behind can be a terrifying experience, and it might heighten your need to fit in with your new surroundings. Even as I packed my bags and got ready to go to college, I was overwhelmed with equal parts apprehension and anticipation.

On that fateful first day, a whirlwind of emotions churned within me. Excitement mingled with apprehension and eagerness warred with anxiety. Stepping into the unfamiliar territory of a new school, I couldn't help but feel overwhelmed by the sheer magnitude of change that lay ahead.

The school's hallways seemed like an intricate maze, with each turn leading to another uncharted corridor. Faces of unfamiliar classmates drifted by, their conversations forming a distant murmur in my ears. The lockers lining the walls stood like sentinels, guarding the secrets of countless students who had walked these halls before me. It was a place of untold stories and endless possibilities, and I was just beginning to find my place within its narrative.

The thought of adjusting to a completely new routine weighed on me like a heavy burden. The comforting predictability of my previous school days had been replaced by a daunting uncertainty. Timetables, teachers, and classroom dynamics were all unfamiliar territory, and I knew that it would take time to navigate this new terrain.

Despite the fear that threatened to hold me back, I clung to a fierce determination. I was resolute in my resolve to make the most of this fresh start and to forge meaningful connections with my peers. The promise of new friendships beckoned, and I knew that overcoming my initial trepidation was the first step towards embracing this exciting chapter in my life.

As I ventured further into the day, my eagerness began to triumph over my apprehension. Each interaction with a fellow student, no matter how brief, was a potential stepping stone toward friendship. The school's vibrant atmosphere and the energy of my classmates became a source of motivation, propelling me forward into the unknown with renewed determination.

In retrospect, that first day, with all its fears and uncertainties, marked the beginning of a transformative journey—one that would ultimately shape not only my academic path but also my character and the friendships that would endure far beyond those initial moments of trepidation.

HOW MY ADDICTION SAVED MY LIFE

While emotions bleed my heart, words pour out instead…

"Jealousy can take hold and take away your control
A poisonous feeling that only serves to take its toll
It makes you doubt yourself and those around you
Making you feel small, unable to break through

But love is an ally that can help you through
It can fill you with comfort and bring a whole new view
It can make you feel strong and powerful too
Showing us beauty that can come from being true

Jealousy is a sickness that's hard to shake
But with love as a guide, it's easier to make
The right decisions that will keep you afloat
And help you reach the goals you wrote

Love will never steer you wrong
It will help you stay strong
And fill you with confidence
So you can be the best version of yourself."

Chapter 3

"The journey of life is not always easy, but it is through our struggles and hardships that we grow and become stronger."

Lamont entered my life through a different avenue. He was the younger brother of my sister's husband, and he lived in South Carolina. I had known Lamont from the time I visited my sister's house. Given that his older brother had married my sister on my father's side, I frequently encountered Lamont during my visits. Our connection developed naturally, born from a sense of family and the familiarity of shared experiences.

Looking back on my experiences, I am filled with a deep sense of gratitude and awe. Life has a way of testing us and bringing us to our knees, but it is through these challenges that we discover our strength and resilience. My story is about love, heartbreak, and, ultimately, forgiveness and growth. Through it all, I have learned that no matter what obstacles come our way, we have the power to overcome them and create a life full of joy, peace, and fulfillment.

Our friendship blossomed into something truly special, and it was during my high school graduation that our relationship took a significant turn. At that pivotal moment, we transitioned from being just friends to something much more profound.

Our bond continued to grow stronger, and it wasn't long before we embarked on a journey that would redefine our lives. Love blossomed between us, and our connection deepened as we navigated the challenges and joys of a committed relationship. It was during this period that we officially started dating, and our love for each other grew with each passing day.

Our love story reached its most beautiful chapter when our son, Naheim, came into the world. Naheim's arrival solidified the love and commitment we shared, adding a new dimension of joy and purpose to our lives. Together, we embraced the responsibilities of parenthood, supporting each other every step of the way.

What began as a friendship evolved into a love story filled with growth, resilience, and the beauty of family. Lamont and I, bound by our shared experiences and unwavering love, continue to build a life together that is both meaningful and filled with love for each other and our son, Naheim.

Lamont was certain that to stop selling drugs for the benefit of our young son, he needed to change his lifestyle. When I was six months pregnant, my partner and I decided to move into an apartment together.

I went into early labor when I was seven months pregnant. I had thought that the contractions I was experiencing were simply Braxton-Hicks until my partner became concerned and started tracking how often they occurred. The labor and delivery process was the most agonizing experience ever.

When we arrived at the hospital, I was already seven centimeters dilated and in severe agony. The doctors informed me that it was too late for an epidural and that the baby would be here soon. As a direct result, I did not get any form of anesthesia or pain medication during my delivery.

Even though the labor was difficult and painful, I had to battle for my child and my marriage this time. We believe that the gift of a child is a blessing from God, and we are thankful beyond words.

Motherhood was a life-changing event and a major factor in my healing process. Becoming a mother brought a sense of purpose and responsibility that I had never experienced before. I was determined to be the best mother I could be and to provide a stable and loving environment for my child. It was a newfound source of motivation and inspiration, and it helped me to let go of the past and focus on the future.

Becoming a parent ushered in a whole new dimension of duty and expansion for me. As we worked our way through the trials and triumphs of co-parenting a child, I gained a wealth of knowledge about myself and my relationship with Lamont. The arrival of our child brought us even closer together, and as the days passed, our love and respect for one another deepened. I am thankful that I was given a chance to be a mother and have the ability to positively influence other people's lives.

In addition to the challenges, parenting also brought much joy and fulfillment. Watching my child grow and develop into their unique person was a constant wonder and amazement. The love and bond that I felt with my child were unlike anything I had ever experienced, and it gave me a new perspective on life and love.

The capacity of love to bring about change is brought home to me as I consider my path. I am thankful for the progress and healing that resulted from the experience, even though I had to overcome many challenges and difficulties along the way. I discovered that it is possible to triumph over challenges of any magnitude by cultivating compassion and forgiveness toward one another and maintaining a dogged commitment to finding solutions.

The tremendous sensation of holding our kid for the first time brought us even closer together, and it was a moment we would never forget. It served as a timely reminder that love and family are the two most essential things in life, as well as the fact that our relationship is worth fighting for.

As we moved forward, I realized the lessons I learned through my experience were invaluable. I learned the importance of communication in relationships and that it's never too late to make things right. I also learned the importance of protecting myself and my partner by always practicing safe sex.

When I consider how far I have come, I am overcome with appreciation and happiness. I will always be thankful to Lamont for his unwavering love and support, which got me through one of the most difficult periods of my life. I want to express my gratitude for the chance to begin over and create a life full of joy and wellness with my loved ones.

I feel a deep sense of gratitude and joy when I think

about how far I have come. The love and support of Lamont were what got me through one of the most difficult times in my life, and I will always be thankful for his unwavering devotion to me. My journey has taught me many lessons about love, forgiveness, and self-care, and I want to share my advice with other women who may find themselves in a similar situation.

It is essential to make time for self-care and introspection regularly. This entails setting aside some of your time to concentrate on your mental, physical, and emotional health. It is easy to forget about yourself and your requirements while dealing with intense feelings, but it is essential to remember that you cannot give from an empty cup. Make sure you schedule time for things that bring you joy and tranquility, such as reading, working out, or spending time with your loved ones and friends.

Additionally, seeking help from loved ones, friends, or a therapist is essential when going through tough times. When you are going through a challenging period in your life, it might be beneficial to have someone you can talk to who can provide you with direction and support. A supporting person in your life, whether a member of your family, a close friend, or a professional counselor, can make all the difference in the world.

The strength that comes from forgiving others is one of the most valuable things I've taken away from my experience. The corrosive effects of harboring anger and resentment towards oneself or others can impede progress and make it impossible to continue. The act of forgiving yourself and others does not imply that the event in question was acceptable; nonetheless, it does make it possible for you to let go of the detrimental feelings and get started on the journey of recovery.

To heal from an error in the past, time, effort, and communication are required. It is essential to remember that making errors is a natural aspect of human existence and that it is never too late to put things right. It is possible to triumph over any challenge and rediscover happiness and love in one's life if one has the correct support and maintains an optimistic viewpoint.

"The road to recovery and happiness may be a long and difficult, but it is worth it when you find peace and love within yourself and with others."

Chapter 4

"Grief is the price we pay for love."

- Queen Elizabeth II

The experience of grief is a natural and normal reaction to a loss, and its manifestations are distinct for each individual. It is not limited to the passing of a loved one but can be experienced in other types of loss as well, such as the end of a relationship, the termination of a career, or the deterioration of one's health. Because it is a multifaceted feeling that can be challenging to absorb and work through, grief cannot be readily expressed or comprehended.

The news from my father that my mother had passed away came crashing down on me like a ton of bricks. My baby boy, Naheim, had just been born, and I was bursting with happiness and anticipation at the prospect of becoming a mother for the first time. However, All those emotions have been replaced at this point by ones of rage, uncertainty, and grief. I was frustrated that I never got to present my mother with the opportunity to meet her grandson. It broke my heart to realize that I would never get another chance to talk to or see my mother again.

In the following days and weeks, I struggled to come to terms with my loss. I felt like I was in a nightmare, and I couldn't shake the feeling that my mother was still alive somewhere. I found myself constantly thinking about her and missing her terribly. I was also struggling to balance the demands of being a new mother with the intense emotions that I was feeling.

As someone who has experienced the loss of a loved one, I can attest to the powerful and complex emotions that come with grieving. I remember feeling overwhelmed with emotions. The waves of these emotions would come and go, often triggered by something as simple as a photograph or a familiar location. At times, my grief felt like it was too much for me to bear. I struggled with my day-to-day life and found it difficult to focus, sleep, and make decisions. Physical symptoms, such as exhaustion, headaches, and stomach problems, also became a part of my experience with bereavement.

I have come to realize that everyone's mourning journey is unique and special. There is no right or wrong way to grieve and no predetermined timeline for when sorrow should end. It may take some years or even a lifetime to come to terms with their loss. And for me, my grieving process has not been a sequential experience but rather a rollercoaster of emotions.

I want to emphasize that it is okay to not be okay. Grief is a challenging and overpowering emotion, but with time and support, it is possible to manage it and find peace.

Lamont and I had fallen in love in a way that seemed almost too good to be true. We had both prayed for someone to come into our lives, and we could never have imagined that a young girl from Philadelphia would find her soulmate in South Carolina. My mother would have been over the moon about our relationship, and she would have been even more excited about becoming a grandmother.

My mother was the strongest member of our family, and we could always count on her to be there for us whether we needed a helping hand or someone to talk to. She never stopped having love and compassion for other people despite the numerous difficulties she had during her life, which included a struggle with drug addiction and schizophrenia.

While I was growing up, I watched how my mother fought off her demons and emerged on the other side more resilient and determined. She had always been a model for me to follow, and I respected her tenacity and her unyielding attitude. As I battled to come to grips with her passing, a question that kept running through my head was why this had to take place. Why did God choose to take her from us in such a heartbreaking way? My mind was constantly racing with questions.

After my mother passed away, I found myself feeling disoriented and isolated, and I had no idea how to proceed with my life. She had been there for me whenever I needed help or reassurance, but now that she wasn't there, I was on my own to figure out how to navigate the world. I looked to my faith for comfort, but the anguish and bafflement were too intense then.

During the time that I spent trying to make sense of these feelings, I concluded that the love and memories that my mother had left behind would remain with me for the rest of my life. She made a tremendously good impact on the lives of a large number of people and the world as a whole. I found a lot of relief and comfort in the thought that all of the suffering and affliction she had been through during her life was finally over and that she was finally free from it.

I decided to focus on the positive recollections I had of my mom and the valuable life lessons that she had taught me throughout the years. I decided that I would honor the legacy she had established in me by loving others, demonstrating compassion, and being kind to those around me. She was the one who instilled in me a sense of appreciation for these things.

Although the grief never truly went away, I learned how to live with it. I learned that feeling angry and sad was okay and normal to experience intense emotions after losing someone you loved. I also learned that reaching out to others for support and talking about my feelings was important. With the help of my husband, family, and friends, I was able to heal and start to build a new life for myself.

"Grief is like a river that carries us through the darkest valleys of our lives."

- Unknown

I was aware that I needed to keep going forward to provide for my family, which consisted of my husband, Lamont, and our two children. I dove headfirst into motherhood, devoting my attention to the care of both Naheim and our daughter, who joined our family at a later time. As the years passed, I discovered solace in the fleeting moments of happiness brought into my life by my children.

During the challenging time I was going through, Lamont was an excellent support system. He was always there to listen, console, and help in any way he could. He was always there for me. I was conscious that his presence was essential to my survival during this ordeal. He was the steady foundation of my life, and I will forever be grateful to him for his love and support.

I found comfort in my children's joy and the purity of their hearts while I was taking care of them. They served as a constant reminder of the beauty in life, and they gave me the motivation to carry on. It was important to me to instill in children the same values that were instilled in me by my mother and to do so in a way that would make her proud.

Lamont and I got married when he was 28 years old and I was 23 years old, and 2 months pregnant with our daughter Patricia. After some time had passed. We had discovered a powerful and unshakable love, and we were also blessed with two lovely children. After relocating from our apartment, our family was finally complete, and we were settling into our brand-new apartment, which was bursting with love and joy.

When I was with my children and sitting on the couch in our new apartment, I had a wave of calm that swept over me. Even though my mother was not physically present, I will always carry the love and energy she gave me. Although I had not yet finished grieving my mother's death, I had an overwhelming sense of optimism toward the future.

Looking out the window at the sky colored in hue, I believed that God was sending me a clue that whatever happens, it will pass. I was filled with a sense of peace. I knew that my mother was watching over us and that she was proud of the family we had become. Life may not have been perfect, but it was beautiful in its way.

I will always miss my mother, but I take comfort in knowing that she is no longer suffering and is in a better place.

"Losing a loved one is never easy, but with love and support, we can find the strength to carry on."

- Unknown

Chapter 5

"Death leaves a heartache no one can heal; love leaves a memory no one can steal."

- Richard Puz

Dealing with your problems and stirring on with your life can be challenging, but doing so will ultimately give you the strength to get back up on your feet.

The process of dealing with trials might be challenging at times. It is not always easy to face the realities of what has occurred, accept them, and find a means to move on when anything traumatic has occurred. However, it is vital to keep in mind that difficulties are an inevitable component of life, and no one is exempt from experiencing them. How we respond to adversity is what ultimately defines who we are and the extent of our capabilities.

It also occurred to me I slipped and fell terribly, but I tried to view every challenge as a chance to learn something new and improve my skills. realized that life is not always what you think it will be because it is unpredictable. Life may be positive even when you believe it will be negative, and it can also be negative even when you are incredibly optimistic about the future.

We moved out of our previous apartment and into a mobile home we rented, but it was rather tough for us to manage our financial obligations. Lamont had been looking for work for several weeks but had been unsuccessful thus far. It came time to pay the rent, but he had little money left. Lamont was experiencing frustration and anxiety, yet he did not quit.

At long last, he was granted an interview at a brand-new establishment, which turned out to be a mechanic shop in the central business district.

As Lamont made his way into the mechanic shop, he was acutely aware of the rapid beating of his heart in his chest. Because he had been rejected by many establishments, he was beginning to lose hope. He inhaled deeply before pushing open the door and heading toward the counter, where the manager was positioned.

Lamont greeted the manager by saying, "Good morning, sir," while extending his hand to shake the manager's hand.

The manager looked up from the stack of papers he

was shuffling, grasped Lamont's hand, and gave it a strong shake before returning his attention to the papers. "Have a nice morning. You must be Lamont, "He replied while glancing at the resume sitting in front of him.

He was being questioned by the manager, a tall man with a clean-shaven head. The manager inquired about the applicant's employment history before asking, "So, you've worked in this business before?"

"Not specifically, but I'm a quick learner, and I'm always excited to give new experiences a shot," Lamont responded, expressing his desire to be hired for the position.

"We only pay minimum wage, so. Are you looking into it? "The manager stated presently.

Lamont had a twinge of disappointment, but he nevertheless nodded in agreement. "Yes, sir. I have an interest in this, "he remarked.

"So, let's go on. You start at seven in the morning tomorrow, "according to the manager.

As Lamont exited the mechanic shop, he experienced feelings of relief as well as gratitude. He knew it was not the job he desired, but at least it was a job, and it allowed him to pay the rent.

Lamont came to the shop the following morning. He rolled up his sleeves and began to clean. The temperature and humidity were high, and he could feel sweat trickling down his forehead. It was a day that was both hot and humid. He was putting in a lot of effort, trying his best to keep up with the fast-paced nature of the establishment, when he suddenly became aware of a voice coming from behind him.

"Hey, man. You are performing quite well here. Hey there, my name is Roy."

When Lamont turned around, he discovered a tall, lanky man beaming broadly from ear to ear. He also wore a gold hoop earring in addition to the tattoo that was on his arm.

"Thanks, guy. Hi there, my name is Lamont. "Lamont said this while experiencing some apprehension due to Roy's outgoing personality.

Next to Lamont, Roy began cleaning, too; Roy finally started asking questions about what they were doing.

"So, tell me, Lamont, where are you from?"

"My roots are in South Carolina. A few months ago, I relocated to this location, "Lamont responded, indicating that he was more at ease now.

"Cool. Although I was born in the North, I've been a resident of this area for quite some time now. You're going to have to put up with a lot here, but eventually, you'll adjust." Roy stated.

After some discussion, Lamont concluded that Roy was a trustworthy individual. He was humorous, generous, and simple to get along with. Lamont and Roy spent a few weeks working side by side, and before long, they had developed a friendship. After work, they would either watch a game at home or go out for drinks together.

Lamont invited Roy and his wife, Christine, to dine with us at our apartment on one occasion. We had a wonderful day, and Lamont and I were delighted he had the opportunity to meet such wonderful people.

As the night went on, Lamont and I couldn't help but feel grateful for the company of Roy and Christine. They had made the evening so enjoyable with their humor and light-hearted conversation. Lamont and I had never felt so comfortable with people we had only recently met.

HOW MY ADDICTION SAVED MY LIFE

Christine had brought along a homemade dessert, which was incredibly delicious, and the conversation over dinner had been lively and engaging. After dinner, we played board games and talked late into the night.

Over the following weeks, Lamont and Roy grew closer, sharing stories about their childhoods and aspirations for the future. They worked well together, and their banter kept them both going during long shifts. Lamont realized that he had found a great colleague and a true friend in Roy.

Lamont's life began to turn around as the months passed by. Roy and Christine were close to both of our children, and as a sign of their happiness, they agreed to be our godparents. Lamont and I thought of them in the same vein as family.

Then, one day, everything was different. A call came on Lamont's phone from the restaurant where he was working. It was the manager, and he was very nervous as he spoke.

"Lamont, I'm afraid I have some very bad news for you. Yesterday evening, Roy and Christine were involved in an automobile accident. They did not succeed in making it, "according to the manager.

Lamont had the sensation that he had been struck by a truck. He was having trouble comprehending what he was being told. It appeared that Roy and Christine had left. Inside, he had a feeling of numbness and emptiness. After hanging up the phone, he slumped on the floor and tried to make sense of everything that had just occurred.

It's hard to remember much about the days that came after. Lamont and I went to the funeral, but we could not bear to look at the deceased's body.

It was as if everything in Lamont's and my worlds suddenly came crashing down on top of him. We were devastated by the loss of friends and people who had become like family. We struggled to come to terms with the catastrophe and its aftermath for quite some time.

The path to wellness for Lamont and me was long and winding, but we eventually felt stronger. The support of his faith community and the kindness of his friends and family helped ease our minds. By relying on our loved ones, we were able to pull ourselves together and start making plans for the future. We knew Roy and Christine would want him to keep moving forward and make the most of every possibility.

HOW MY ADDICTION SAVED MY LIFE

Lamont found consolation in reflecting on his time with Roy and Christine. He remembered all the good times they had shared, including the many laughs, meals, and games they had shared.

Lamont sought solace in the recollections of his friends Roy and Christine as he sat in the peace and alone of his home. He couldn't help but crack a grin as he recalled how Christine would always be there to lend an attentive ear and a comforting embrace and how Roy would always make everyone laugh with his lame jokes. He was aware that losing his loved ones would make a hole in his life, but he was also aware that the love and kindness they had shown him would be with him for the rest of his life.

Lamont was well aware that his life would change significantly in the absence of Roy and Christine, but he also recognized that he had been extraordinarily fortunate to have them as a part of it. He vowed to keep their legacy alive by making people happy and living his life to the fullest, just as they had done for him. He also vowed to be as nice to others as they had been to him. As a result, Lamont found solace in the recollections of his dear friends, secure in the knowledge that the love they had for him would never leave him, even in their absence.

The reality of life is that we will all face challenges. When something terrible occurs, it is not always simple to face the realities of what has occurred, accept those realities, and find a way to move on. However, it is essential to remember that our identity and the limits of our ability are shaped by how we react to adversity.

"The reality is that you will grieve forever. You will not "get over" the loss of a loved one; you will learn to live with it. You will heal and rebuild yourself around the loss you have suffered. You will be whole again, but you will never be the same. Nor should you be the same, nor would you want to."

- Elisabeth Kubler-Ross

Chapter 6

"The world breaks everyone, and afterward, some are strong in the broken places."

- Ernest Hemingway

I would often wake up with a knot in my stomach, feeling like I was carrying a heavy weight on my shoulders. The world around me would seem dull, and even the simplest tasks felt like an insurmountable obstacle. But I kept telling myself that I had to be strong and couldn't let anyone see how I was truly feeling. So, I would smile and go about my day, all the while feeling like I was barely holding on.

I would try to distract myself from my thoughts by immersing myself in work or taking care of my family. But even those activities would sometimes feel like a chore. My depression had a way of seeping into everything, tainting even the brightest moments with a feeling of gloom.

It was like I was walking on a tightrope, with the smallest gust of wind threatening to knock me off balance. And so, I kept my emotions carefully locked away, hoping no one would notice the fragility beneath the surface.

Deep down, I knew it was only a matter of time before I would break. I could feel the pressure building, like a volcano ready to erupt. And yet, I was so scared of what would happen if I allowed myself to be vulnerable.

The world around me had become a blur, and even the simplest things could trigger a wave of emotions I couldn't control. I would try to hold back tears, but sometimes, they would spill over, leaving me feeling even more exposed.

As a child, I was always aware of my mother's mental health struggles. She would have days where she couldn't get out of bed or moments where she would see things that weren't there. It was like she was living in a world that only she could see, and it scared me.

I became more determined to distance myself from her struggles as I grew older. I thought that by pretending everything was okay, I was somehow avoiding the same fate. So, I kept my depression hidden, hoping no one would see the turmoil beneath the surface.

The guilt of my actions weighed heavily on my mind. The affair had been a mistake, and I knew it had deeply hurt my partner. And then there was my mother's death, which left me feeling numb. I couldn't understand why I wasn't more affected by it or couldn't bring myself to cry like everyone else.

I tried to push these feelings away, burying them deep inside of me. But the more I did, the more the guilt ate away at me. It was like I was carrying around a heavy weight that was slowly crushing me.

I thought that by not expressing my depression, I was somehow being strong. But in reality, I was like a time bomb, just waiting for the moment when everything would come crashing down.

Lamont was my pillar of strength during the toughest times of my life. His unwavering support and love were like a soothing balm for my soul, bringing me comfort and calm amid the storm.

Unlike me, he didn't have any mental health issues. He was always so level-headed and in control, never letting his emotions get the best of him. He was like a beacon of stability, shining brightly in the midst of my darkness.

Despite his steadfastness, I still couldn't open up to him about my struggles. It was like there was a wall between us, one that I had built with my insecurities and fears. I didn't want to burden him with my problems or risk being judged for my weaknesses.

So, I kept everything bottled up inside, pretending everything was okay even when it wasn't. I put on a brave face, smiling through the pain, all the while knowing that I was slowly unraveling.

Our children were the light of my life, the reason I woke up every day with a renewed sense of purpose. They were our pride and joy, and we did everything in our power to give them the life they deserved. We showered them with love and attention, always making sure they felt valued and cherished. I was terrified of what would happen if I let it out, afraid that it would somehow taint the happy life we had built for our children.

I didn't want my children to grow up in an environment where mental health issues were stigmatized or where fear ruled their lives. I wanted them to know that it was okay to feel sad or anxious and that it was a natural part of being human. But I also didn't want them to see me struggling; I didn't want them to bear witness to the darker parts of my soul.

So, I kept my depression hidden, locked away in a dark corner of my mind. And while I knew it wasn't a healthy way to live, I couldn't bear the thought of burdening my children with my struggles.

The financial strain did cause some disagreements between Lamont and me, but it never affected our relationship. We knew that our love was stronger than any material possession and that we could weather any storm as long as we had each other.

The weight of my depression was becoming too heavy to bear. It was like a heavy blanket suffocating me, making breathing hard. Every day felt like an uphill battle, and I ran out of strength to keep going. I was on the verge of a nervous breakdown, and I knew it.

I kept my struggles hidden, not wanting to burden Lamont or anyone else with my problems. I didn't want to be seen as weak, and I didn't want to be a burden to anyone. So, I put on a brave face, pretending that everything was okay, even though I was slowly unraveling on the inside.

As the days went by, the pressure continued to build within me. My thoughts became a jumbled mess, and my emotions were everywhere. I was like a pot of boiling water, ready to boil over at any moment. And yet, I still couldn't bring myself to admit that I needed help.

It wasn't until I was at my breaking point that I finally broke down and confided in front of Lamont. And even then, it wasn't easy. I was afraid of what he might think or say, scared that I might lose him if I showed him the true extent of my pain.

He surprised me with his compassion and understanding. He listened patiently as I poured out my heart, holding me close and letting me know that everything would be okay. He didn't judge or criticize me but offered me his unwavering support and love.

At that moment, I realized how lucky I was to have him by my side. He was more than just my husband - my partner, friend, and confidante. And while my journey towards healing was far from over, I knew I had him to walk with me every step.

With Lamont's support, I sought professional help for my depression. It wasn't easy, and sometimes I wanted to give up, but I knew I couldn't let my mental health issues define me. It was a slow and gradual process, but I began to feel like myself again over time. The guilt and shame weighing me down for so long slowly dissipated, and I started to see a glimmer of hope for the future.

As I continued working through my issues, I realized I had been wrong about vulnerability. It wasn't a weakness; it was a strength. By admitting my struggles and seeking help, I had taken a brave step towards healing. And with Lamont and our children by my side, I knew that I could overcome anything.

Lamont took the initiative in the days that followed, conducting research to find the most qualified therapists and counseling services for me. Even though it required some of his own time and energy, he went out of his way to ensure that I received all of the assistance I required to emerge victorious from my depression. He was my black stallion, and I understood that I was extremely fortunate to have him at my side at all times.

As I took the first steps toward my recovery, I noticed that I was beginning to view the world through a new lens. The sounds were more lively, and the colors appeared to be more colorful. When I allowed my despair to take control of my life, I soon understood how much I had given up because of it. I was able to find the resolve to face my issues and ultimately triumph over them with Lamont's unflinching support.

When I think about it now and look back, I realize how much my worry about being like my mother prevented me from achieving my goals. Nevertheless, I am also aware that I am not my mother and that it is perfectly acceptable for me to seek assistance when I am in need of it. I am more powerful than I have ever been before, and it is all owing to the love and support that I have received from Lamont.

As I move forward on my path, I am gaining the wisdom to treat myself with more compassion and to stop stuffing my feelings deep within me in favor of feeling them and working through them. I am making going to therapy and taking care of myself a priority as part of my efforts to prioritize my mental health. It's a fight I have to fight every day, but I'm determined to come out on top.

I hope that by sharing my story, others will know that they are not alone in their struggles. That there is no shame in seeking help and that vulnerability is not a weakness but a strength. As I reflect on my past and look toward the future, I am reminded of a quote by Maya Angelou, *"I can be changed by what happens to me. But I refuse to be reduced by it."*

Chapter 7

"The world breaks everyone, and afterward, some are strong in the broken places."

- Ernest Hemingway

I would often wake up with a knot in my stomach, feeling like I was carrying a heavy weight on my shoulders. The world around me would seem dull, and even the simplest tasks felt like an insurmountable obstacle. But I kept telling myself that I had to be strong, that I couldn't let anyone see how I was truly feeling. So, I would put on a smile and go about my day, all the while feeling like I was barely holding on.

I would try to distract myself from my own thoughts by immersing myself in work or taking care of my family. But even those activities would sometimes feel like a chore. My depression had a way of seeping into everything, tainting even the brightest moments with a feeling of gloom.

It was like I was walking on a tightrope, with the smallest gust of wind threatening to knock me off balance. And so, I kept my emotions carefully locked away, hoping that no one would notice the fragility beneath the surface.

Deep down, I knew that it was only a matter of time before I would break. I could feel the pressure building, like a volcano ready to erupt. And yet, I was so scared of what would happen if I allowed myself to be vulnerable.

The world around me had become a blur, and even the simplest things could trigger a wave of emotions that I couldn't control. I would try to hold back tears, but sometimes, they would spill over, leaving me feeling even more exposed.

As a child, I had always been aware of my mother's mental health struggles. She would have days where she couldn't get out of bed or moments where she would see things that weren't there. It was like she was living in a world that only she could see, and it scared me.

As I grew older, I became more determined to distance myself from her struggles. I thought that by pretending that everything was okay, I was somehow avoiding the same fate. So, I kept my depression hidden, hoping that no one would see the turmoil that lay beneath the surface.

The guilt of my actions weighed heavily on my mind. The affair had been a mistake, and I knew that it had hurt my partner deeply. And then there was the death of my mother, which left me feeling numb. I couldn't understand why I wasn't more affected by it, why I couldn't bring myself to cry like everyone else.

I tried to push these feelings away, burying them deep inside of me. But the more I did, the more the guilt ate away at me. It was like I was carrying around a heavy weight that was slowly crushing me.

I thought that by not expressing my depression, I was somehow being strong. But in reality, I was like a time bomb, just waiting for the moment when everything would come crashing down.

Lamont was my pillar of strength during the toughest times of my life. His unwavering support and love were like a soothing balm for my soul, bringing me comfort and calm in the midst of the storm.

Unlike me, he didn't have any mental health issues. He was always so level-headed and in control, never letting his emotions get the best of him. He was like a beacon of stability, shining brightly in the midst of my darkness.

Despite his steadfastness, I still couldn't bring myself

to open up to him about my struggles. It was like there was a wall between us, one that I had built with my own insecurities and fears. I didn't want to burden him with my problems or risk being judged for my weaknesses.

So, I kept everything bottled up inside, pretending everything was okay even when it wasn't. I put on a brave face, smiling through the pain, all the while knowing that I was slowly unraveling.

Our children were the light of my life, the reason I woke up every day with a renewed sense of purpose. They were our pride and joy, and we did everything in our power to give them the life they deserved. We showered them with love and attention, always making sure they felt valued and cherished. I was terrified of what would happen if I let it out, afraid that it would somehow taint the happy life we had built for our children.

I didn't want my children to grow up in an environment where mental health issues were stigmatized or where fear ruled their lives. I wanted them to know that it was okay to feel sad or anxious and that it was a natural part of being human. But I also didn't want them to see me struggling; I didn't want them to bear witness to the darker parts of my soul.

So, I kept my depression hidden, locked away in a dark corner of my mind. And while I knew it wasn't a healthy way to live, I couldn't bear the thought of burdening my children with my struggles.

The financial strain did cause some disagreements between Lamont and me, but it never affected our relationship. We knew that our love was stronger than any material possession and that we could weather any storm as long as we had each other.

The weight of my depression was becoming too heavy to bear. It was like a heavy blanket suffocating me, making it hard to breathe. Every day felt like an uphill battle, and I was running out of strength to keep going. I was on the verge of a nervous breakdown, and I knew it.

I kept my struggles hidden, not wanting to burden Lamont or anyone else with my problems. I didn't want to be seen as weak, and I didn't want to be a burden to anyone. So, I put on a brave face, pretending that everything was okay, even though I was slowly unraveling on the inside.

As the days went by, the pressure continued to build within me. My thoughts became a jumbled mess, and my emotions were all over the place. I was like a pot of boiling water, ready to boil over at any moment. And yet, I still couldn't bring myself to admit that I needed help.

It wasn't until I was at my breaking point that I finally broke down and confided in front of Lamont. And even then, it wasn't easy. I was afraid of what he might think or say, scared that I might lose him if I showed him the true extent of my pain.

He surprised me with his compassion and understanding. He listened patiently as I poured out my heart, holding me close and letting me know that everything was going to be okay. He didn't judge me or criticize me but instead offered me his unwavering support and love.

At that moment, I realized just how lucky I was to have him by my side. He was more than just my husband - he was my partner, my friend, and my confidante. And while my journey towards healing was far from over, I knew that I had him to walk with me every step of the way.

With Lamont's support, I sought professional help for my depression. It wasn't easy, and there were times when I wanted to give up, but I knew I couldn't let my mental health issues define me. It was a slow and gradual process, but over time, I began to feel like myself again. The guilt and shame that had been weighing me down for so long slowly dissipated, and I started to see a glimmer of hope for the future.

As I continued to work through my issues, I realized that I had been wrong about vulnerability. It wasn't a weakness; it was a strength. By admitting my struggles and seeking help, I had taken a brave step towards healing. And with Lamont and our children by my side, I knew that I could overcome anything.

Lamont took the initiative in the days that followed, conducting research to find the most qualified therapists and counseling services for me. Even though it required some of his own time and energy, he went out of his way to ensure that I received all of the assistance I required to emerge victorious from my depression. He was my black stallion, and I understood that I was extremely fortunate to have him at my side at all times.

As I took the first steps toward my recovery, I noticed that I was beginning to view the world through a new lens. The sounds were more lively, and the colors appeared to be more colorful. When I allowed my despair to take control of my life, I soon understood how much I had given up because of it. I was able to find the resolve to face my issues and ultimately triumph over them with Lamont's unflinching support.

When I think about it now and look back, I realize how much my worry about being like my mother prevented me from achieving my goals. Nevertheless, I am also aware that I am not my mother and that it is perfectly acceptable for me to seek assistance when I am in need of it. I am more powerful than I have ever been before, and it is all owing to the love and support that I have received from Lamont.

As I move forward on my path, I am gaining the wisdom to treat myself with more compassion and to stop stuffing my feelings deep within me in favor of feeling them and working through them. I am making going to therapy and taking care of myself a priority as part of my efforts to prioritize my mental health. It's a fight I have to fight every day, but I'm determined to come out on top.

I hope that by sharing my story, others will know that they are not alone in their struggles. That there is no shame in seeking help and that vulnerability is not a weakness but a strength. As I reflect on my past and look toward the future, I am reminded of a quote by Maya Angelou, *"I can be changed by what happens to me. But I refuse to be reduced by it."*

Chapter 8

"Although the world is full of suffering, it is also full of the overcoming of it."

- Helen Keller

As I reflect on my past decisions, a sense of regret washes over me like a tidal wave. I can't help but feel a deep sense of sorrow for the ways in which I let my sadness control my life. It was a difficult and frightening period, one that I never thought I would be able to survive. But somehow, I managed to pull through, and it was during this time that I came to realize just how much my marriage and the friends and family who supported me truly meant to me.

Looking back on those dark days, I remember feeling lost and alone, as if I was drowning in a sea of despair. The weight of my sadness was almost too much to bear, and I felt like giving up at times. But even in the midst of my pain, I knew that I couldn't let it consume me completely. I had to hold on to something, anything, that would help me find my way back to the light.

It was during this period that I turned to my loved ones for support. They were my anchor, my rock, and my safe haven in the storm. I leaned on them for strength and comfort, and they never let me down. Their unwavering love and support helped me to see that I wasn't alone and that I had people in my life who truly cared about me.

As I emerged from the darkness and began to see the light once more, I felt a renewed sense of gratitude for my marriage and my loved ones. They had been with me every step of the way, offering their love and support even when I couldn't see the path ahead. And it was this love that gave me the strength to keep moving forward, even in the face of adversity.

As I think back to that difficult period in my life, I remember the few people who stood by me through it all. One of those people was my coworker, Stan. We worked together at the engine distribution company, and he was always willing to lend an ear when I needed to talk.

At first, I appreciated his support. But as time went on, I began to notice that he was a bit too friendly with me at times. I found myself talking to him on the phone more often than I should have been, and his constant attention made me feel uncomfortable. Although there was nothing sexual between us, I started to feel uneasy about the amount of attention he was giving me.

Looking back on it now, I realize that this was the first clue that I was beginning to slide into a state of depression. My energy levels were low, and I had a difficult time finding joy in things that used to bring me pleasure. I started to withdraw from my friends and family, and I felt as if I was alone in the world.

In some ways, I think that Stan sensed this change in me. Perhaps he thought that he could help me by being extra supportive, but his over-friendliness only made me more aware of how isolated I was feeling. It was a strange dynamic, and I wasn't sure how to handle it.

As I look back on that difficult time, I can't help but remember the strain that my interactions with Stan placed on my marriage. My husband, Lamont, was understandably unhappy with the way I was talking to him on the phone and confiding in him about my personal struggles. Although there was nothing romantic or sexual between us, Lamont interpreted it as a betrayal, and it caused him a great deal of pain.

I tried to explain to Lamont that nothing was going on between Stan and me, that I was just talking to him as a friend. But my words fell on deaf ears, and the trust that we had built over years of marriage was damaged. It was difficult for him to believe me and to rebuild the trust that had been broken.

I could see the pain in Lamont's eyes, and it broke my heart. I knew that I had hurt him deeply, and I desperately wanted to make things right. But I didn't know how to rebuild the trust that we had lost. It seemed like every conversation we had ended in tears or anger, and I felt like we were drifting further apart.

As we worked to rebuild our relationship, Lamont would often ask me to explain what was going on inside of me. He wanted to understand the root of my depression and why I had turned to someone else for support. But despite his persistence, I found it difficult to put into words what was happening inside of me.

My emotions were complicated, and I didn't even fully understand them myself. I was struggling with feelings of sadness, hopelessness, and despair, and I didn't know how to break free from them. The weight of my depression was suffocating, and it seemed like no matter how hard I tried, I couldn't shake it.

HOW MY ADDICTION SAVED MY LIFE

Lamont could see the pain that I was in, but he didn't know how to help me. He wanted to be there for me, to support me through my struggles, but he didn't know what to do. And as much as I wanted to open up to him, I couldn't find the words to express what was going on inside of me.

It was a frustrating and isolating time for both of us. I felt like I was drowning in my own emotions, and Lamont felt helpless to save me. But even though we couldn't fully understand what was happening, we knew that we had to work through it together.

We leaned on each other for support, even when we didn't know what to say or do. Slowly but surely, we began to make progress. The weight of my depression started to lift, and I began to see a glimmer of hope on the horizon.

Our children, Naheim and Patricia, were only 8 and 5 years old at the time, respectively. Naheim was a sensitive child, and he could sense that something was wrong with me. He would often ask me about the source of my distress, his eyes welling up with tears as he tried to understand what was happening.

As a mother, it was heartbreaking to see my child in such a state of distress. I wanted to protect him from the pain that I was feeling, but I didn't know how. And as Lamont and I talked more about our situation, we realized that we needed a fresh start.

We needed to create a new beginning for ourselves and our family. We couldn't keep going on like this, weighed down by the burden of my depression and the strain it was putting on our relationships. We needed to find a way to move forward, heal the wounds that had been inflicted, and start anew.

It wasn't an easy decision to make, but we knew that it was the right one. We needed to take a step back, reassess our priorities, and make changes where necessary. And as we began to take those first steps towards a new beginning, we could feel the weight of our burdens start to lift.

Despite the fact that we had discussed the possibility of moving before, it had never been a serious consideration for us. We had built a life in South Carolina with our jobs, our friends, and our community, and we couldn't imagine leaving it all behind.

But as we faced the reality of our situation, we knew that something had to change. We couldn't let our marriage fall apart, and we couldn't let our children continue to suffer because of our struggles. We needed a fresh start, a new beginning that would allow us to rebuild our lives and our family.

So, after much discussion and deliberation, we made the difficult decision to uproot our family and leave the state of South Carolina. It wasn't an easy decision to make, and we knew that it would come with its own set of challenges, but we also knew that it was the best thing for us.

We spent months researching different cities and towns, weighing the pros and cons of each location, and considering all of the factors that were important to us. We wanted a place where we could start over, where we could build a new community, and where we could create a life that was better than the one we had before.

And finally, after much searching, we found a place that felt right. A place where we could start fresh and build a new life together. It was scary and exciting all at once, but we knew that it was the right decision.

We were on the fence between going to Atlanta or Florida, but in the end, we decided to go to Florida. We wanted to wipe the slate clean and leave everything in the past, including the painful recollections that had taken over our lives. We were aware that this was the only option available to us if we wanted to keep our marriage and our family together, but it was not an easy one to make.

The move to Florida served as the necessary therapy for the two of us. It was a fresh start, a chance to put our problems in the past and begin again with a clean slate. We were bound and determined to make it work, but we were also aware that if it didn't, we would have to discuss the possibility of getting a divorce.

As we prepared to leave our previous life behind and began to pack our belongings, I couldn't help but feel a wave of helplessness rush over me. I had no idea what the future would bring, and the uncertainty filled me with dread. Yet I was also aware that I needed to keep my composure, both for the sake of my loved ones and for my own sake.

The trip to Florida was a long and difficult one, but on the bright side, it allowed us all plenty of opportunities to talk about what had happened and what we were looking forward to in the future. We shared our concerns and uncertainties as well as our hopes and dreams during our conversation. We shared our sorrows and our joys, as well as our commitment to always be there for one another, no matter what.

The moment we touched down in Florida, it felt like someone had taken a burden off our shoulders. The sky was clear, and the air was pleasant and inviting despite the sun's presence. We were prepared to seize this fresh start, this opportunity to begin again, and we saw it as such.

"What lies behind us and what lies before us are tiny matters compared to what lies within us."

- Ralph Waldo Emerson

Chapter 9

As we looked around our new apartment, we couldn't help but feel a sense of pride for what we had accomplished. It was a small space, but it was ours, and we were determined to make it a home. However, the reality of our financial situation soon set in. We had very little furniture, and our limited income meant that we had to be frugal with our spending.

Despite the challenges, we were grateful for the roof over our heads. The apartment may have been small and sparsely furnished, but it was a place to call our own. We were determined to make the most of what we had and create a comfortable living space for our family.

Lamont had recently started a new job at Midas, and we were hopeful that it would provide the financial stability we so desperately needed. However, the first few weeks had been tough, and the bills were starting to pile up. The news that our Blazer had been repossessed was a blow, and we knew that we had to find a way to make up the shortfall in our finances.

As I got out of bed and headed to the kitchen to start breakfast, I noticed something was off. The driveway was empty, and our car was nowhere to be seen. It was then that it hit me: our car had been repossessed. I couldn't believe it. I knew that things were tough, but I never imagined that our car would be taken away from us.

The thought of Lamont having to walk five miles to work each day was a daunting prospect. He was already putting in long hours at Midas, and the extra challenge of the daily commute on foot was going to be tough on him. However, it was during one of these walks that he met Andrew, who would turn out to be our angel in disguise.

Andrew's kindness didn't end with just a few rides and groceries. As it turned out, he was a mechanic who worked with Lamont at Midas, and they had only known each other for two weeks. But when Andrew overheard Lamont's conversation with his manager about our struggles with rent, he didn't hesitate to offer his help.

The next day, Andrew came over to our apartment with $600. It was a significant amount of money for us, and we were incredibly grateful. We had been struggling to make ends meet, and his generosity had given us a glimmer of hope that things would get better.

Andrew had also brought with him some beautiful

furniture. A puffy sectional that reclined and had a table in between the sections, complete with vibrating features. It was like a dream come true. We had been sitting on the floor, and the idea of having comfortable furniture seemed like a luxury we could never afford. But Andrew's kindness had given us a new lease on life.

The passage of time made it very clear that Andrew was more to Lamont than merely a colleague at the workplace. Their acquaintanceship had developed into a profound tie, and it was obvious that Andrew had become more than just a buddy; he was essentially Lamont's brother from another mother. Outside of work, they would frequently spend time together, and Andrew had become a constant presence in our lives as a result of this.

It was incredible to think that someone we had only known for a short period of time could be so thoughtful and generous. We will be eternally thankful to Andrew for his generosity and compassion, which helped us get through some of the most difficult times in our lives, and we will miss having him around. Because of the extraordinary efforts he had made on our behalf, we counted ourselves quite fortunate to have come into contact with him.

Andrew's kindness wasn't just reserved for us. He was the type of person who would go out of his way to help anyone in need. His generosity extended to his friends, family, and even strangers. He was truly an inspiration and a testament to the power of kindness.

It's incredible to see how one person's kindness can have such a significant impact on someone's life. Andrew had not only helped us through our struggles, but he had also shown us the importance of being kind and compassionate towards others. His kindness had created a ripple effect that had touched the lives of everyone he had come into contact with.

In a world where negativity and division seem to dominate, Andrew's kindness was a shining light that reminded us of the goodness in humanity. We will always be grateful for his presence in our lives and the impact that he had on us.

The generosity of Andrew had lifted a significant burden off our shoulders. With the rent paid and some beautiful new furniture in our apartment, we could finally breathe a little easier. It was a relief to know that we wouldn't have to worry about being evicted from our home.

In addition to Andrew's help, we were also approved for food stamps, which helped us put food on the table. It was a difficult decision to apply for government assistance, but we knew that we needed it to survive. The food stamps gave us a bit of breathing room and allowed us to focus on our other needs.

Another blessing came in the form of the Boys and Girls Club. Our children had been accepted, and it was a real joy to see them make new friends so quickly. The Club provided a safe and supportive environment where they could learn, play, and grow. It was heartwarming to see the smiles on their faces as they ran around, playing and laughing with their new friends.

As parents, it was a huge relief to know that our children were happy and thriving despite the challenges we were facing. The Boys and Girls Club had given them a sense of community and belonging, which was incredibly important during such a difficult time in our lives.

Our living arrangement in the gated community was a true blessing. It was a world away from where we had started, and we were grateful for every little thing. The small apartment with its basic furnishings was more than enough for us. We had a roof over our heads, a warm bed to sleep in, and a kitchen to cook our meals.

As the days turned into weeks, we began to settle into our new routine. The stress of our financial situation started to fade away as Lamont worked hard to provide for us. He would come home exhausted from work, but he never complained. His dedication and hard work were a source of inspiration for us all.

It seemed like things were finally coming together. Our bills were being paid on time, and we even managed to put a little money aside for a rainy day. We had learned to live within our means and appreciate the little things in life. We no longer took anything for granted and were grateful for every blessing that came our way.

Lamont's faith in God had always been a guiding force in his life, and during this difficult time, it seemed like it was strong enough for both of us. His unwavering belief in a higher power gave us a sense of hope and comfort that was hard to describe.

We had been through a lot, but we were grateful for the little blessings that came our way. Each day brought new challenges, but we faced them with a sense of determination and faith that things would get better. We prayed for strength and guidance, and it seemed like our prayers were being answered. It was a testament to the power of faith, hard work, and the kindness of strangers.

As time passed, we began to settle into our new life. My children had made new friends at the Boys and Girls Club, and it was heartwarming to see them so happy. They looked forward to going every day, and it was a relief to know that they were in good hands.

Lamont's performance at work was up to par, and the two of us had reached a point where things were going in the right direction. The difficulties with money that used to dominate our lives are a thing of the past now. We had traveled a significant distance from where we had begun, and we were pleased with how far we had progressed.

After going through so much difficulty, it was a blessing to finally be in a position of success. We no longer felt as if we were carrying the weight of the world on our shoulders, and instead, we were finally able to take a deep breath. We had acquired the skills necessary to live within our means, take joy in life's simple pleasures, and put forth consistent effort in pursuit of our objectives.

The fact that we were able to triumph over such a difficult time period is evidence of both our resiliency and our dogged drive. We had met the challenges that life threw at us head-on and emerged from those encounters more resilient.

We were thankful for the experiences that had taught us valuable lessons, as well as the support of people who had assisted us along the way.

"I can be changed by what happens to me. But I refuse to be reduced by it."

- Maya Angelou

Chapter 10

Life felt like the deepest scar, acquiring to be healed, asking for unspoken help when the addiction took hold of me. It felt like a vice, slowly squeezing the life out of me. I never thought I would become addicted to anything, let alone inhaling carburetor cleaner and gasoline. But as the years passed, the addiction took over my life, and my personality changed. I found myself with three personas, each one distinct and battling for control.

Tashonda was an intelligent and hardworking mother and wife, striving to keep up appearances and maintain a facade of normalcy. Sasha was a tough and intimidating personality, always ready to fight and never back down. And then there was Chloe, a scared and timid nine-year-old I could only talk to in secret.

As my addiction spiraled out of control, my family began to notice the changes in me. They saw me slurring my words and acting strange, and I would get defensive and angry when they questioned me. But deep down, I knew I had lost control and needed help.

Concealing my addiction initially and then hiding it for a long time overwhelmed me and gave me a lot of anxiety. My addiction had taken a severe toll on my body, and the foul odor emanating from my pores was impossible to ignore. This resulted in me being fired from several jobs.

The inhaling carburetor cleaner would cause me to experience intense periods of nodding, during which I would slip into a trance-like state. I would sometimes even lose consciousness while on the toilet at work.

The first time I hit rock bottom was when I realized I was messing up with remembering numbers when I was extremely good at it. I realized something was seriously wrong when I started having trouble remembering simple things like what I ate for breakfast. My inability to recall important information became increasingly concerning, and it was then that Lamont realized that I was struggling with addiction.

My addiction got to a level that I started to cheat to complete my satisfaction. I once resorted to theft to obtain the carburetor cleaner that had become a necessary addiction. At the time, I was so consumed by the desire to satisfy my addiction that I didn't hesitate to steal 2 to 3 cans from an auto store, even going so far as to pawn off valuable jewelry that belonged to both myself and my loved ones for a meager $20.

I was in a dark place. My body had become immune to the effects of carburetor cleaner, so I began drinking it in the hopes of achieving that intense high I craved. Eventually, I even started mixing gasoline with the cleaner and taking shots of the dangerous concoction. It became a daily routine, with me inhaling five cans of carburetor cleaner and drinking a pint of the mixture daily for a year.

I lost control of my bodily functions, waking up to find feces and urine all over the bed. I was also experiencing vision problems, and an eye doctor told me that the nerves in my eyes had been damaged by the toxic substances I had been ingesting. Despite the clear health risks, I couldn't stop. The rush was just too intense.

The addiction caused me to have anxiety attacks, and I would have to breathe into a paper bag to calm down. The high was short-lived, so I constantly chased the next fix. My family was gone during the day, so I had the house to myself to indulge in my dangerous habit. I didn't care about the risks; all I wanted was the next high.

My husband Lamont, working as a mechanic and making good money, had to put me on his insurance because I had been fired from every job. We grew apart, and my kids no longer trusted or respected me. They even started calling me by my first name.

My sense of smell and vision deteriorated rapidly, to the point where I couldn't even detect the aroma of freshly popped popcorn or sizzling bacon. I struggled to distinguish between green and red, leading me to run numerous red lights. Due to these concerning developments, Lamont intervened and confiscated my car keys. As a result, I no longer have access to a vehicle.

I was in terror, confusion, and anger when my son discovered me lying face down on the ground with my glasses shattered. It was a direct consequence of my worsening eyesight, which had progressed to almost total blindness, requiring me to wear glasses. Unfortunately, my declining mobility skills and deteriorating muscle strength caused me to fall face-first onto the ground, damaging my glasses and the injuries sustained in the fall.

I am a parent who unfortunately struggled with addiction to inhaling cans, which caused serious breathing problems for my son, who has asthma. Despite my son's health issues, my desire to inhale the cans was strong, and I would hide them around the house to ensure I always had a supply. This behavior caused my son's condition to worsen to the point that he had to use his inhaler more frequently, ultimately leading to him calling the police on me.

I know that my addiction was harmful to my son and my family, but I found it difficult to resist the temptation to inhale. Unfortunately, my addiction led me to be arrested and sent to a rehabilitation center that was more like a prison than a place of healing. Despite my initial attempts at recovery, I relapsed and ended up back in rehab.

After my second stint in rehab, I was determined to overcome my addiction and make positive changes in my life. I secured a job and worked hard to maintain my sobriety. However, my addiction had already taken a toll on my marriage, and my husband Lamont had asked me for a divorce. I understood that my actions had hurt him and our family, and it was difficult for me to come to terms with the consequences of my addiction.

I have always had a strong intuition as a woman, and it was on high alert when my husband Lamont started coming home late and leaving again soon after, even though his car remained in the driveway. I called his workplace to try and talk to him, but he told me that his job did not allow employees to use their cell phones. I understood, but my intuition was still nagging at me.

Lamont's birthday was approaching, so I surprised him by buying tickets to a Neo Soul concert. I thought we had a good time, but after the show, we ate, and Lamont left as soon as we got home. The next morning, I checked Lamont's cell phone records on our shared family plan and saw that he had been calling the same number repeatedly for hours on end. This was strange because he had told me he couldn't make phone calls at work. I called the number, and it was his ex-girlfriend Shana.

Lamont and Shana had been together before I moved to South Carolina, and we never got along. As I confronted Lamont, I asked him, "Why were you talking to her in the first place? And why did you keep it a secret from me?"

Lamont replied, "Listen, I saved her life. She was about to commit suicide, and I talked her out."

His response took me aback, and I couldn't believe what I had heard. I retorted, "Are you serious? Are you going to choose her over me? She's just some random girl, and I'm your wife!"

Lamont tried to reason with me, "No, it's not like that. I care about you. But I couldn't let someone take their own life."

I was furious and snapped back, "Let the bitch die. I can't believe you care more about her than your wife."

I remember that day like it was yesterday. It was April 2, 2016, and my life was falling apart. Lamont, the man I thought loved me, had betrayed me in the worst possible way. I had just found out that he had been confiding in his ex-girlfriend, Shana, about my addiction. And to top it off, he refused to tell me why Shana had tried to kill herself.

I was so angry and hurt I couldn't even think straight. "How could he do this to me?" I yelled, pacing back and forth in my living room. "After everything I've been through, he tells her about my addiction. And they're Facebook friends? Are you kidding me?"

My son was in the room with me, looking concerned. "Mom, please calm down," he said. "I don't want you to relapse again."

I couldn't calm down. I felt like my whole world was crashing down around me. "I don't know what to do," I said, tears streaming down my face. "I feel so betrayed. And now I'm going to relapse again because of this."

Suddenly, there was a knock at the door. It was the police. My son had called them again, and this time, he had gotten an injunction order against me for 24 hours. I was furious. "What the hell?" I yelled. "I can't even go in and get my shoes and debit card? My son asked me to help him pay his phone bill, and I gave him my card. I need it back."

The cop just shook his head. "I'm sorry, ma'am, but I can't allow you to go in there. You're not allowed to have any contact with your family for the next 24 hours."

I felt so helpless. Lamont was at work, and I had nowhere to go. "Please, can't you just throw me my shoes and card?" I pleaded with my daughter when she cracked open the door.

She just looked at me with disgust. "No, Naheim told me not to give you anything. You're not welcome here anymore."

I was shocked. My own family had turned against me. I felt like I was losing my mind. "What am I supposed to do?" I cried.

I hid in the shed in the backyard, hoping that Lamont would come home soon and rescue me. But instead, the police showed up and arrested me for violating the injunction. I was taken to jail, and I could feel myself spiraling out of control.

The jail was a nightmare. I was going through withdrawals and felt like I was losing my mind. I got into fights with other inmates, and I was thrown into solitary confinement for 24 hours. It was the lowest point of my life.

I went without food by choice for a few days while in jail, but it wasn't by choice. I was then handed a manila envelope by one of the COs. I took the papers out and read them. It was divorce papers from my husband, Lamont. I saw that he would have to pay me alimony, which I knew he couldn't afford. I felt a mix of anger and betrayal, but most of all, I felt like I had been thrown away like garbage. He couldn't sell the house without me, as my name was on the deed. I couldn't believe he was leaving me for that "bitch, Shana."

At that moment, I tore the papers in half and threw them away. How dare he try to divorce me? I didn't eat much while in jail, and I was warned that if I didn't eat, I would be put on suicide watch. So, I traded my food for apples and bread. The COs woke us up at 5 a.m. for the count. Breakfast was at 6 am, lunch was at 12 pm, and dinner was at 5 pm. If you didn't have a commissary, that was all you got. But the inmates could make gourmet out of anything.

One day, it was my turn to ride on the jail bus to court. I was shackled and handcuffed with the other inmates. When I entered the courtroom, it was filled with people. A video was playing about an injunction. I didn't know what was happening, but I knew I would soon find out.

Sitting there, I saw my son enter the courtroom with an attorney. He was dressed in a black suit as if he was attending my funeral. The judge spoke and then gave me a chance to say something. I said nothing. Then, the judge asked my son how long he wanted the injunction to last. I will never forget his words, "Indefinite."

The judge ruled that the injunction would be indefinite, and my son and his attorney left the courtroom. Lamont wasn't there, only my son. That was the day I felt like I had died inside. I was broken beyond fixing. I had no family from that day on.

I called my sister and stepmother from jail, and they

told me that my family had packed my belongings and were waiting for me. I was in prison for 35 days and was served with divorce papers while there. It was twice that I read and ripped up the divorce papers. After that, I got into fights with other inmates. I didn't care about anyone or anything. I had nowhere to go and no family.

I remember one day, an inmate put her finger in my food. I snapped and broke her nose with my tray. I was put in the hole for three days. Those days were rough because I was withdrawing and throwing up almost daily.

"I don't care what happens to me anymore," I muttered to myself.

Chapter 11

Stepping out of the jail gates, I knew I was alone. The bus stop seemed like the only viable option for me. The Lynx bus arrived, and without hesitation, I got on it. It was a surreal feeling, riding a bus alone in a city I once called home. I had no destination in mind, but somehow, I found myself on the same street where my family lived.

The thought of seeing my children and husband gave me a sense of comfort, but I knew it was unlikely. The injunction they had filed against me was still in place, prohibiting me from contacting them. Nonetheless, I had to try. I knocked on the door, and to my surprise, my daughter answered.

What I saw next was a sight that broke my heart. My belongings were packed, and my daughter had been waiting for me to arrive. It was evident that my family had given up on me. The feeling of betrayal was overwhelming. How could they abandon me? How could my husband, who vowed to stand by me through thick and thin, leave me when things got rough?

With my debit card and my last paycheck, I had $1,200 in my name. It wasn't much, but it was all I had.

I remember that day vividly, the day when I had nothing left to live for. It was a dark and stormy day, and my mind was clouded with despair. I decided to go to the auto store to get some carburetor cleaner, something to help me forget my problems. The UBER driver dropped me off, and I loaded up the basket with about 20 cans of the stuff. I didn't care about anything else, not even my own safety.

The driver dropped me off at a hotel, where I unpacked and started inhaling the fumes. It was like I was at my own party, but I knew deep down that this was a dangerous game I was playing. I was a mere 112 lbs., and my body couldn't handle the toxic fumes for much longer. But I didn't care. My family had deserted me, and God didn't seem to give a shit about me, so why should I care about myself?

Days passed by in a blur as I inhaled and slept, barely conscious of the world around me. But on the third day, hunger pangs woke me up from my stupor. I stumbled out of the hotel and found myself lost in the rain. I was soaked to the bone and shivering, but I couldn't find the pizza shop I was looking for.

I saw what looked like a shortcut through a fenced

area, but there was a sign that read "Keep out." I didn't care; I was desperate and wet. I went through the opening in the fence, but before I could take another step, I was electrocuted and thrown about 30 feet. I landed on the broken pieces of rock, feeling a searing pain in my left leg.

I don't remember much after that except stumbling upon a Disney tourist store. The manager saw me and asked if I was okay. I must have looked like a mess. I told him I was trying to find my hotel, and he immediately got me a fresh, dry shirt to wear.

"You're bleeding," he said, pointing to my leg.

I looked down and saw a big gash on my left leg, just below my knee. I must have sustained it during the electrocution. I didn't even feel it until now.

"Why didn't you let me die?" I muttered to myself, feeling angry at God.

The manager called an ambulance for me, and I was rushed to the hospital. I survived, but I was left with scars, physical and emotional. I never dared to go back to the hotel or the Disney store. I was too ashamed to face the people who had helped me when I was at my lowest.

I had cans of carbonator cleaner waiting for me when I arrived at the hotel. I left the lobby and made my way to my room, determined to get high once again. The feeling of the fumes entering my lungs was like nothing else, and I didn't care about anything else at that moment.

Days went by in a blur, and I couldn't even remember eating during that time. The only thing I knew was that I needed to inhale more of the carbonator cleaner. I would wake up on the floor, my nose bleeding through the night. I didn't even realize that I had a gash on my leg until I saw the dried blood on my face and the soaked sheets.

Then, there was a knock on the door. I stumbled over to it and opened it to find people in hazmat suits standing there. I was so high that I thought they were astronauts at first. They asked me questions like who the president was and what the date was, and I struggled to answer them. They bandaged my leg and told me that I needed stitches, but I refused.

As they cleaned the blood from my face, the hotel manager kicked me out. The police were there, and they told me I couldn't come back. I packed my things and walked across the street to another hotel. I looked like a homeless person with garbage bags full of clothes and a blanket.

As I stood there, I realized that my pants were soaked with urine. I couldn't control it, and I felt humiliated. A man around my age approached me with a Bible in his hands. He squatted down and started to pray for me. I didn't want to hear it, and I told him what I thought about his God. But he didn't give up. He continued to pray, even as I rolled my eyes and tried to walk away.

After he finished, he left me with the words, "God loves you and will never forsake you." I didn't believe him, but his words stuck with me. I booked a room for one night at the hotel across the street, still in my pee-soaked pants. It was all I could afford.

I wasn't concerned about the next day; I just wanted to get back to my room so I could start inhaling again. Luckily, I had stashed an extra can in my rolling suitcase since the police had taken the one that I had left on the hotel table. I spent the next three to four hours furiously inhaling until Lamont called me. By that point, my brain was completely fried, and I could barely remember my own name.

"Where are you at?" Lamont asked when he called.

I struggled to remember where I was staying but eventually managed to give him the name of the hotel. Within an hour, he arrived to pick me up. I assumed that we were going home, but instead, Lamont told me that he was taking me to South Carolina to see my father.

My memory got hazy after that, but Lamont filled me in on what happened. Apparently, I had fallen into a stupor during the drive, and when I woke up, I didn't even recognize Lamont.

"Mister, where are you taking me?" I kept asking him over and over again.

Lamont didn't answer, and I began to cry. I told him that my mother was making waffles and that she had asked me to go outside to get the puppy so that I could eat. It was clear that I was lost in some sort of delirium.

After a while, I fell asleep again. When I woke up, I asked Lamont where we were going once more, but he didn't respond. I was starting to panic, so I called my sister.

"I'm in a car with a man, and I don't know where we're going," I told her.

"Where's Lamont?" she asked me.

"I don't know," I replied.

Lamont took the phone from me and explained the situation to my sister. He told her that he was taking me home to see our father.

I can hardly put into words the confusion and disorientation that overwhelmed me as I drifted in and out of consciousness. Lamont, my husband, later recounted to me how I would wake up crying and calling him "Mister," not even recognizing my own partner. In my delirium, I would ask him where we were going, but he remained silent, staring straight ahead at the road ahead of us. I later learned that he was asking God why this was happening to his beloved wife.

At times, I would become more lucid, briefly regaining some awareness of my surroundings. I would tell Lamont that I had to get home to my mother, who was making pancakes for breakfast, and that I needed to bring in our puppy. But then I would break down in tears and slip back into unconsciousness.

Eventually, we arrived at my sister's house, and I awoke to find myself in a strange place, surrounded by unfamiliar faces. I stepped out of the car, but I had no idea where I was or who these people were. My brother-in-law approached me, and I started shaking and crying uncontrollably. My sister asked me what was wrong, but I couldn't answer. Lamont had to explain to her that I didn't even recognize my own family.

My father held me, and I could see the hurt and confusion in his eyes as he asked me if I knew who he was. I didn't, and it broke my heart to see the pain that my temporary memory loss was causing my loved ones. My sister eventually took charge and told me to lie down, and I must have slept for a couple of hours.

When I awoke, I stumbled outside to where everyone was gathered, still feeling disoriented and unsure of what had happened. My sister greeted me, and I could see the relief in her eyes when I responded to her as though nothing had ever happened. But I had no memory of the past few hours, and I didn't even know that Lamont had brought me to South Carolina to stay with my father.

It was a dark and lonely time for me. Lamont, my husband, had just left me at my father's house in South Carolina, claiming he was doing it to save my life. But I didn't believe him. All I could think about was how much I hated this place and how much I missed my family. I begged

Lamont not to leave me, but he didn't listen. As he drove away, I cursed God for letting this happen to me.

I felt like I was in a nightmare, sitting on the sofa in my father's house, surrounded by strangers. Lamont had already left, not even saying goodbye. My father, Louie, showed me to my room and told me not to unpack until the morning. But I couldn't sleep. I stayed up all night watching TV, feeling numb and alone.

The next morning, I was still in shock. My father treated me like a child, laying down rules and checking my purse whenever I left the house. I couldn't believe how powerless I felt. That night, I couldn't take it anymore. I went into the kitchen and slit my wrist with a knife. It wasn't sharp enough to do any real damage, but I didn't care. I just wanted to escape.

The next thing I knew, my mother was sitting next to my bed, looking at me with concern and sorrow in her eyes. My mother passed away over 20 years ago, but there she was, sitting right next to me. I spoke to her in a low voice, blaming her for everything that had happened. And then she was gone.

The following few months were a blur. I was depressed and missing my husband and children, but I couldn't contact them because of the injunction. My father's wife, Lori, treated me like a maid, and my father did nothing to stop her. I felt like a prisoner in their house.

One day, my younger sister invited me to stay the night with her, and surprisingly, my father allowed it. I packed a few things, including some cotton balls, and left the house.

As we drove to my sister's house, I was struck with disbelief at the sight of an automotive store we passed by. Despite the gravity of my addiction, my sister made no inquiries, and we simply enjoyed each other's company, reveling in the joy of being sisters. However, the prospect of acquiring more of the substance loomed large in my mind, and I couldn't help but wonder how I could get to that auto store.

The next day, my sister informed me that she would be taking her son to his father's house but would not be gone for too long. As we spent the night talking and laughing, I knew that I had to seize this opportunity to get my hands on more of the substance. After waiting for about 30 minutes, I made my way to the auto store armed with a can of carburetor cleaner.

As I walked back to the apartment, I began inhaling

the contents of the can with reckless abandon. It was like a breath of fresh air, and I couldn't get enough of it. At times, I would even spray the chemical directly into my mouth like a can of cheese whip. I was in a euphoric state and barely even noticed the walk back. Half the can was gone, but I was determined to inhale every last drop of it.

Upon my arrival at the apartment, my sister was still out, and I took advantage of this opportunity to indulge further. I was so consumed by the substance that I lost consciousness and woke up disoriented, having gotten lost on my way back to the apartment. Thankfully, I managed to find my way back, but not before nearly depleting the can of carburetor cleaner.

When my sister finally returned much later, I was already passed out, but I had the presence of mind to hide the can before succumbing to the effects of the substance.

The next day, I arrived at my father's house, and my sister dropped me off. As soon as I walked in, my father demanded to search my belongings for any signs of contraband. Despite feeling violated, I knew I had nothing to hide and reluctantly allowed him to proceed.

After a thorough search, my father found nothing,

and I could sense the relief in his demeanor. However, my mind was still clouded from the previous night's escapades. I couldn't shake the feeling that my sister suspected something.

As soon as I was alone in my room, I retrieved the can from the sleeve of my jacket and stashed it under my mattress.

As I lay in my bed that night, the weight of my vice on my conscience became heavier with each passing moment. I knew that what I was doing was wrong, but I couldn't resist the lure of the can hidden in my room. As I took deep drags, my mind raced with guilt and fear, but the pleasure of the high was too intense to resist.

The next morning, I awoke to the sound of my father's wife's angry voice. The pungent aroma of the can's contents had alerted her to my transgression. As she stormed into my room, I knew I was in trouble. I tried to deny the existence of the can, but she was relentless in her pursuit. After an exhaustive search of the trash can, I finally admitted to the truth and retrieved the can from its hiding place.

My father's wife wasted no time in reporting my behavior to my father, who was working hard as a longshoreman. He arrived home furious and demanded to know where I had obtained the can.

I lied and said I had walked to the store to get it, but deep down, I knew I had let him down.

I was ashamed and wanted to get rid of my addiction, but I kept my desire to satisfy myself always a priority!

Chapter 12

"Rock bottom became the solid foundation on which I rebuilt my life."

- J.K. Rowling

A heavy sense of unease settled in my chest as I reluctantly disclosed the truth, a truth I had hoped to shield from prying eyes and meddling hands. The question he posed was innocent enough, harmless in its simplicity, but the answer weighed upon me like an anchor, threatening to drag me into a realm of unwanted vulnerability. I had no choice but to surrender to the truth, for I valued honesty above all else.

He asked me a question that I really didn't want to involve my sister in, but I had no choice but to tell him the truth. I was at my sister's house when he informed me that as long as I stayed at his place, I would need to be supervised. I didn't take that news lightly at all. The following days were agonizing; I felt like a grounded teenager once again.

One day, when my dad was at work, and Louisa had gone to pick up her grandkids from school, I took a walk toward the shed located at the back of the house. My father had a decent-sized boat parked there. As I entered the shed,

I searched for anything I could inhale, desperate to escape my emotional turmoil. I stumbled upon a container that emitted a strong odor resembling nail polish remover. Curiosity got the better of me, and I inhaled deeply until I felt lightheaded. It was a sensation I had never experienced before, and strangely, I found myself drawn to it. Without thinking, I consumed some of the liquid but quickly realized my mistake as I began to choke and gag. I desperately held my throat, unable to swallow the dangerous substance.

Gasping for air, I hurried back to the house, panic setting in. I grabbed my phone and dialed 911, but I couldn't utter a word. I could hear the operator on the other end of the line. Just then, Louisa's grandson entered the house and spotted me. He immediately called out for his grandmother's help. By that point, I had lost consciousness.

When I regained consciousness, I found myself in the hospital, my father standing beside me, his eyes filled with a mixture of fear and disappointment. What I had unknowingly consumed turned out to paint thinner, obstructing my airways. The medical team had to pump my stomach to remove the toxic substance. They suggested admitting me to a psychiatric ward, but my father insisted on taking Care of me at home.

The passing weeks melded together in an indistinct haze as if I were confined within the walls of a prison. Solitude remained elusive, for my father and his wife engaged in ceaseless arguments day in and day out. She claimed to be retired, though how one could retire from nothingness eluded my comprehension. With my father toiling away long hours and dedicating himself to his band, aptly named Hush, he was seldom present at home. This absence served as a catalyst for their frequent discord. I loathed my existence within those walls, and I found myself wishing I had met my demise rather than endured this wretched nightmare.

One evening, my father arrived home clutching a peculiar kit containing Q-tip swabs and two minuscule containers. He informed me that it was a drug test kit, as though he presumed me to be devoid of intellect. But I remained silent, aware of the unmistakable appearance of such a kit. We each took a Q-tip and methodically swabbed our respective jowls, depositing the swabs within the tiny containers. That night, tears streamed down my face as I drifted into a fitful slumber, plagued by the burning question of why God harbored such disdain for me. What had I done to merit such a merciless fate?

Some hours later, roused from my somnolent state, I

discovered my mother seated on the floor before me, her legs crossed in an Indian-style position. Her countenance exuded a peculiar serenity, yet sadness lingered within her eyes. Not a single word escaped her lips, and we remained locked in a silent gaze. I yearned for her to utter even a syllable, hoping for solace in her voice. Unable to bear the silence any longer, I beseeched her, questioning the reason behind God's apparent animosity toward me. I implored her to relay my message of abhorrence to the divine, expressing my own intense hatred. And just like that, she vanished into the ether, leaving me bereft once again.

On a seemingly ordinary day, while engrossed in television's mind-numbing glow, a text message illuminated my phone's screen. Anticipating yet another calamity, I braced myself for the contents of the message. To my astonishment, the text displayed an image—a photograph of a piece of paper adorned with meticulous print. I had to enlarge it to decipher the minuscule words.

The paper bore the inscription: "PATERNITY RESULTS." Puzzled, I scrutinized the document, my eyes coming to an abrupt halt upon encountering the phrase "99.9% negative." Nevertheless, I continued reading as if hoping the words might miraculously change their meaning. Alas, they remained unyielding. Louie, the man I had called my father, was, in fact, not my biological progenitor. The magnitude of this revelation overwhelmed me, and to compound the cruelty, this coward had the audacity to communicate the truth via text message. Such cowardice stripped him of the fundamental decency to face me in person, a fact made all the more unbearable considering we shared the same abode.

To make matters worse, I was forbidden from reaching out to my beloved husband, trapped in isolation without any means of solace. If there was ever a shred of doubt in my mind, it has been obliterated now—God, without a doubt, harbors an abhorrence for my very existence.

I didn't lay eyes on Louie, the man I believed to be my father, until the following evening. He entered the room without uttering a word, settling himself in the kitchen area while I occupied the living room. From my peripheral vision, I could sense his intense stare fixed upon me, brimming with an unmistakable animosity. The negative energy he exuded seemed to suffuse the very air around us. Determined to avoid confrontation, I kept my gaze locked on my phone, steadfastly refusing to meet his demonic eyes. This unnerving standoff persisted for about two hours, leaving me to wonder why he harbored such disdain toward me. Was it because he held me responsible for not being his biological daughter? Eventually, he abruptly rose, departing with a resounding slam of the front door. His wife remained secluded in her room throughout the entire episode.

The next morning, faced with a dire choice between life and death, I realized that remaining in that house would inevitably lead to my demise within a matter of days. Gathering my resolve, I retrieved my phone and embarked on a search for rehabilitation facilities. Unfamiliar with the geography, I cared not for the location; all I knew was that I had to escape the horrors of that twisted abode and leave South Carolina behind. My fingers scrolled tirelessly, the image of my mother's face etched in my mind. In a hushed plea, I whispered, "Mom, please help me." Almost as if, in response to my desperate entreaty, a rehab center materialized before me. I dialed the number, tears streaming down my face, confined to the sanctuary of my room.

A gentleman named Steve answered the call, and through choked sobs, I laid bare my addiction and the dire circumstances surrounding me. Compassionately, Steve assured me that reaching out was the right decision, and he requested my insurance information. Being still covered by my husband's insurance, I promptly provided the details. Steve pledged to call me back within ten minutes. True to his word, he dialed my number, revealing that he had arranged a flight for me the following day.

The flight information swiftly landed in my inbox, and with a heartfelt expression of gratitude, I ended the call. Emerging from my room, I awaited Louie's return, steeling myself for the crucial conversation that lay ahead. An hour passed before I summoned the courage to inform him that I was heading to rehab and would be departing the next day. He simply stared at me, inquiring about the destination. I admitted my lack of knowledge, prompting him to demand the phone number of the facility. Relieved that Steve answered, Louie proceeded to interrogate him, peppering him with countless questions and asserting his desire to be involved in every aspect. Once Louie's inquiries were satisfied, we finally disconnected.

Silence reigned between us as I retreated to my room, swiftly packing my belongings with a sense of urgency. There was no time for farewells; all I yearned for was an escape from that wretched environment. Asking Louie if he could drive me to the airport, we embarked on the journey without exchanging a single word. Arriving at the terminal, he accompanied me as far as he could, reaching into his wallet to slip me $50, gently planting a kiss on my forehead. And with that, he turned and walked away, marking the final time I laid eyes on or conversed with Louie.

The flight was incredibly smooth, spanning a mere two hours. Upon my arrival in West Palm Beach, Florida, I found myself unfamiliar with this place. However, to my relief, there stood a gentleman holding a sign bearing my name. Naturally, I assumed he was one of the rehab facility's workers. Introducing himself as Aaron, he exuded a pleasant demeanor and graciously helped load my luggage into the sleek, all-black Escalade SUV.

During our drive to the rehab center, Aaro enthusiastically outlined the myriad amenities it had to offer. He spoke of a private chef who prepared delectable breakfast, lunch, and dinner options. Moreover, there was an open snack bar stocked with a vast array of treats, ranging from cereals to frozen dinners, fruits to soda machines. He even mentioned the presence of a skilled masseuse on the premises. Additionally, the facility boasted a refreshing swimming pool and versatile sports courts for tennis and basketball. His vivid descriptions painted an enticing picture, although deep within, the sting of the divorce papers served by Lamont lingered. While fleeting thoughts of Lamont's involvement with Shana tried to intrude, I swiftly dismissed them from my mind.

Upon reaching the rehab center, I was immediately struck by its grandeur. It resembled a magnificent mansion, leaving a lasting impression on me. Together, Aaron and I unloaded my luggage and proceeded inside, where we were instructed to await the nurse. Soon enough, a kind-hearted nurse arrived and introduced herself. She, too, efficiently took charge of my luggage, explaining the mandatory inspection process. She also recorded my weight, which measured 112 pounds, with my clothes on. Following some paperwork, she escorted me to my room, providing a comprehensive tour of the splendid facility. As Aaron had promised, it exceeded my expectations.

The rehab center housed individuals of diverse ages and ethnic backgrounds, forming a vibrant community. When the nurse inquired about my addiction, I candidly shared my struggles. To my surprise, she regarded me with a baffled expression as if I possessed two heads. Wondering what caught her attention, I asked her directly. She confessed that while she had encountered various addictions, mine was entirely unfamiliar to her. She marveled at my very existence and the fact that I hadn't become reliant on oxygen. Proposing medication to alleviate withdrawal symptoms, she genuinely seemed concerned. However, I firmly declined her offer, not wishing to embark on a discussion about faith or divine intervention. Sensing my reluctance, she tactfully shifted the conversation, handing me a schedule of daily meetings I was expected to attend.

The group sessions proved to be an aspect I disliked immensely. Sharing personal details with strangers was out of the question for me. Consequently, this routine persisted for approximately two weeks. My mind often wandered back to the home I once had, preoccupied with the turmoil caused by my impending divorce. Truthfully, I hadn't sought out rehab to overcome my addiction; rather, it was a last resort when I had nowhere else to turn. The facility became a temporary refuge where I could lay my head and find sustenance. My younger sister occasionally covered my cell phone bill, and I relied on the kindness of others to maintain that lifeline. Despite the presence of diverse addicts, none seemed to share a similar dependency to mine. Growing weary of their tales, I finally mustered the courage to share my own. To my surprise, I was met with a mix of bewilderment and inquiry. While they regarded me as though something was inherently wrong with me, they themselves were in rehab for different yet comparable reasons.

The program encompassed three distinct stages: PHP, the initial phase where leaving the facility was prohibited; IOP, granting some freedom to venture outside and even find employment, albeit with a curfew; and IOP II, a stage that allowed supervised leaves and required drug testing upon return. My goal was to progress to IOP, so I decided to play the game and actively participate, adhering to their requirements. Gradually, I made strides and eventually advanced to the IOP phase. Strangely, I didn't fully grasp the progress I was making, mostly because I didn't care.

Often, I would venture out alone, claiming that I needed time to reflect. In reality, my aim was to search for automotive stores or any place that sold auto supplies. One day, I stumbled upon a Walmart. Casually, I entered the store and discreetly opened a pack of cotton pads, taking about five for myself. With purpose, I made my way to the automotive department, where I found the sought-after carbonator cleaner. Removing the cap, I sprayed the cotton pad and inhaled right then and there, utterly disregarding any consequences. I was past the point of caring. Stealthily, I carried the can to the bathroom, concealing it in my sleeve before making my exit.

Inhaling deeply, I reveled in the familiar euphoria, relishing the long-missed high. Halfway through the can, my elation was cut short as nausea overwhelmed me, leading to an abrupt bout of vomiting. It was a sensation I had never experienced before. Yet, a larger predicament arose—where could I hide the remaining half of the can? Disposing of it was out of the question, and I had neglected to wear a jacket for concealment. My only option was to stash it under a robust bush alongside the building, promising to retrieve it and finish it off the next day.

Returning to the facility, I felt invigorated. I even treated myself to a massage, which provided a temporary respite from my inner turmoil. The following morning, I hastened to the spot where I had hidden the can, retrieving it and stealthily stashing it in my drawer among my clothes. That day, we had our regular meeting sessions, along with a change of scenery for variety. Naively, I felt assured, secure in the knowledge that I could be safely concealed. However, my complacency was short-lived.

Approximately an hour into the session, a lady entered the room and requested that I accompany her. Puzzled and filled with worry, I followed her, contemplating if something had happened to Lamont or the children. She led me to her office, where she presented her phone, displaying an incriminating photo. There, in all its damning glory, was a picture of the can I had hidden in my drawer. With a heavy heart, she informed me that there was nothing more the current facility could do for me. In disbelief, I was ushered to a waiting room, where my belongings had been packed, signaling my expulsion. I had been unceremoniously kicked out, and my anger boiled within me at the thought of being unable to finish the rest of my can.

As a consequence, I was transferred to a psychiatric rehab facility. Deep down, I couldn't shake the feeling that I didn't truly belong there. Witnessing the disconcerting behavior of fellow residents only heightened my unease. One young man, seemingly no older than eighteen, burst out of his room completely naked, sprinting down the corridor before colliding forcefully with a window. Within seconds, a team of orderlies subdued him, administering a tranquilizer to calm him down. His limp body was then carried back to his room.

In another disconcerting incident, a woman who appeared to be in her early twenties sat on the sofa before suddenly contorting herself, hanging upside down from the back and crawling across the floor like a twisted creature from a horror movie. The scenes I witnessed sent shivers down my spine, and the strict monitoring and locked doors only intensified the feeling of captivity. The towering twenty-foot-high walls served as a constant reminder of the lack of freedom within these walls. I found myself confined to this environment for a seemingly endless two weeks, subjected to scrutiny and evaluations by the facility staff and doctors.

Finally, the day arrived when I was deemed fit for release. Within half an hour, a 16-passenger van pulled up, and behind the wheel sat a sharply dressed man who introduced himself as Kyle. Accompanying him was a tall white gentleman named Jeff. They greeted me with the utmost courtesy and without prying into my past. They explained that they worked for a halfway house called We Care, and they promptly assisted me in gathering my belongings.

Despite their reserved nature, their professionalism and politeness were evident. It was a refreshing change from the judgment and scrutiny I had faced in the previous facility. They asked no intrusive questions and allowed me some space to process my thoughts and emotions. As we embarked on the journey, a mix of uncertainty and hope swirled within me. The road ahead seemed long and arduous, but I couldn't help but feel a glimmer of optimism for a fresh start.

"Sometimes the hardest part isn't letting go but rather learning to start over."

- Nicole Sobon

Chapter 13

"The only way out is through."

- Robert Frost

We Care, a facility owned and operated by a married couple named Shawn and Janet, was an establishment I found myself in. They were truly wonderful individuals, and their genuine kindness was evident. From the outside, We Care appeared like a spacious single-story house, boasting seven bedrooms, two bathrooms, a laundry room, a remarkably large kitchen, and an even grander living room with a magnificent 75' television. It resembled a regular home, and despite having a total of eight people, including myself, it never felt cramped. Furthermore, We Care also had another property, a charming cottage-like house located about half an hour away. This secondary location exuded a warm and inviting ambiance, capable of accommodating a family of four. These residences were a far cry from what one would typically associate with a halfway house.

Upon my arrival, I made the decision to embark on a cold turkey approach to my recovery, adamantly refusing any medication assistance. This proved to be the most arduous and agonizing experience I had ever encountered. It felt as though I was plagued by a relentless stomach virus for an excruciating 30-day period. I spent my days incessantly vomiting, even when there was nothing left to expel. Devoid of the ability to retain water, I began to succumb to hallucinations. The patterns on the walls appeared to detach themselves and float aimlessly, while the very structure itself seemed to close in on me. Even the innocent depictions of animals on the shower curtains became animated, engaging in a whimsical chase. It was an incredibly taxing journey, but I managed to persevere, albeit at the cost of further weight loss, bringing me down to a mere 110 pounds.

The staff at We Care were incredibly supportive throughout my ordeal. However, there was one individual named Kyle who commanded a certain level of respect. He displayed exceptional kindness and was always willing to go above and beyond for others. Yet, he approached his job and the pursuit of our sobriety with unwavering seriousness. The treatment program was divided into three stages: Partial Hospitalization Program (PHP), Intensive Outpatient Program (IOP), and IOP II. Personally, the specific stages held little significance to me, as the environment itself never felt confining. Stepping outside felt akin to venturing out into my own neighborhood. I often found solace sitting in the rear section of the house, tucked away from the main area.

Right from the start, I developed a strong bond with my fellow clients. We engaged in daily meetings, with the PHP sessions running from 9 a.m. to 3 p.m. The IOP sessions followed a shorter schedule, lasting from 9 a.m. to 12 p.m. Meanwhile, IOP II only required attendance at meetings twice a week, as many clients had secured employment opportunities. This relaxed pace allowed me to find comfort in my surroundings. My therapist, Robert, played a pivotal role in my recovery journey. It was nearly impossible not to open up to him, and we shared a profound connection. Robert happened to be transgender, and our rapport was truly remarkable.

It had been approximately a year since I last had any contact with Lamont, my partner, and my children. Communication with them was strictly forbidden, but I longed for some reassurance that they knew I was alright. I approached Robert with this request, hoping he could at least reach out to Lamont on my behalf. He explained that such contact would be possible later in the program, but understandably, I would not be present during the conversation. Despite this, I appreciated Robert's willingness to help bridge the gap between us.

While the majority of the facilitators at We Care were amicable, there was one exception – Kayla. A middle-aged woman hailing from Georgia, Kayla had a demeanor that irked me from the very beginning. She, too, was a recovering addict, and her own troubled past included engaging in street prostitution while being married and having a child. Kayla seemed fixated on prying open my emotional vault, constantly urging me to shed my protective barriers. Her persistent proclamations of "stop hiding" and asserting that recovery was a selfish journey focused solely on oneself grated on my nerves. I tried to explain my struggle in comprehending such an approach, emphasizing my intention to return home to my family.

However, Kayla didn't mince her words, suggesting that there was a possibility my family might not accept me upon my return. This ignited a fiery rage within me, and without a second thought, I unleashed a torrent of curses directed squarely at Kayla. At that moment, I completely lost control of my emotions, disregarding the presence of other clients who looked on in disbelief. Their attempts to calm me down were met with my furious outburst, as my anger had consumed me entirely.

The aftermath of that encounter left me feeling a profound mix of regret and embarrassment. The nickname "T" that the clients had given me was now used as a plea for me to regain composure. I realized that I had allowed Kayla's provocations to trigger an outburst that was not only uncharacteristic of me but also disruptive to the harmony within the program.

I find myself harboring immense anger towards her, primarily because deep down, I knew she was right. With each passing day, I found myself consumed by thoughts of Lamont. I would compulsively check his Facebook page multiple times throughout the day. His countenance appeared exhausted and sorrowful as if he barely slept. A bottle of liquor was always within his reach. However, what struck me the most was his relationship status, which read "Separated." Those words pierced my heart, tearing it apart. The disbelief remained overwhelming, even as I was served with divorce papers. It was an unfathomable reality to accept.

Kayla, on the other hand, refused to back down. She persistently confronted me, day after day, in an attempt to break down my defenses and encourage me to open up. What pushed me over the edge was her unwavering Love for God and her relentless pursuit to have us attend her church. In response, I vehemently rejected her proposition, defiantly telling her that neither she nor her God could affect me. This heated exchange persisted for about two weeks.

During this time, my therapist, Robert, informed me that he had tried contacting Louie, whom I had designated as an emergency contact. Robert wished to update him on my progress, but Louie claimed to be too occupied with work to engage in conversation. Recognizing that Louie might not be beneficial to my recovery, Robert suggested that it would be wise to remove him from the emergency contact list. I agreed with his assessment. Robert also mentioned that he had reached out to Lamont, who expressed satisfaction with my progress. Robert proposed the idea of conducting a family session to aid in our healing process, as he believed I was making significant strides. Unfortunately, Lamont declined the offer.

At this point, I found myself emotionally depleted. It had been two months since I last indulged in my addiction, and I was drained both mentally and physically. One day, while sitting on the back porch swing, alone as the other clients enjoyed the beach, I stared up at the sky. Tears began to stream down my face uncontrollably, my emotions overwhelming me completely. At that moment, I gazed upward and spoke to God despite our differences and my vehement resentment towards Him. I acknowledged that I could not hold onto my family and simultaneously fight for my sobriety. A choice had to be made. So, amidst my hysterical crying, with a runny nose and all, I faced an excruciating decision.

I had to decide which aspect of my life to surrender to God, the same God I despised and held responsible for everything I had endured. I realized that, in order to seek help and survive, I had to give my family to Him. With immense difficulty, I entrusted my husband, Lamont, my son, Naheim, and my daughter, Patricia, into God's Care. It was undoubtedly the most challenging thing I had ever done. I relinquished my family and forced myself to forget about each of them, focusing solely on my own well-being. I had to place my trust in God, the very deity I had adamantly rejected, to protect and provide for my loved ones.

The day I surrendered my family to God marked the beginning of how my addiction became the catalyst for saving my own life.

It has been an entire year now, and I must say, things were going quite well for me. I had established a Sunday tradition of cooking for my unconventional family, whipping up dishes like jerk chicken, potato salad, green beans with ham hocks, and upside-down pineapple cake. Occasionally, I'd switch up the menu to keep things interesting. Life seemed to be falling into a rhythm until that one fateful day when I received a call from Lamont.

HOW MY ADDICTION SAVED MY LIFE

I hesitated before answering the phone, a mix of fear and anticipation rushing through me. Lamont's voice, however, lacked any emotional inflection as he informed me that he would have to remove me from his insurance coverage. His company was making cutbacks, and he could no longer afford to keep me on. I was at a loss for words, unsure of what to make of this news. It was through his insurance that I was able to stay at We Care, so I pleaded with him, explaining my progress and the fact that I had achieved a year of sobriety.

Regrettably, my desperate pleas fell on deaf ears. Lamont remained resolute, stating that I would have to find another way to maintain my residence at We Care. The call abruptly ended, leaving me in a state of shock. Seeking solace, I confided in Kayla, my newfound mentor. She reassured me, urging me not to worry too much. Kayla extended an invitation for me to attend her church, believing it would be beneficial for me. Although hesitant at first, I eventually agreed, as Lamont's constant reminders to find an alternative solution weighed heavily on my mind. After all, what did I have to lose?

The following Sunday, true to my word, I accompanied Kayla to church. To my surprise, it was nothing like I had expected. The service began promptly, and to my delight, they even served a substantial breakfast—bacon, eggs, sausage, grits, and coffee. What's more, the entire church proceedings lasted only an hour! I found myself thoroughly impressed by the pastor, an elderly gentleman in his late sixties who exuded wisdom and charisma. I couldn't help but wonder if he had been associated with the Black Panthers during his younger days. He possessed an undeniable smoothness.

The choir and musicians were nothing short of awe-inspiring. Despite my best efforts to resist, I found myself clapping along and tapping my feet to the uplifting melodies. Each time I caught myself, I quickly ceased my movements. Yet, no matter how hard I fought against it, I couldn't suppress the stirring emotions that threatened to well up inside me. The sermon centered around releasing negative energy and surrendering to a higher power. I scoffed inwardly, thinking, "Yeah, right." But I silenced the skeptical voice within me, reminding myself to shut up and listen. Perhaps there was something to be gained from this message.

As time passed, I began attending church regularly. It turned out to be the same place where Shawn and Janet worshiped. Three months slipped by without a single call from Lamont, much to my relief. In all honesty, as the days turned into weeks, I started to feel an unfamiliar sense of contentment. I felt liberated. Christmas was fast approaching, and the staff at We Care brought in a tree and decorations to infuse the home with festive cheer. We all pitched in, decorating the house together. In my eyes, we were like a family—dysfunctional, yes, but a family nonetheless. We were all we had.

Then, out of the blue, Lamont called. I chose not to answer the phone. I was in a good place, finally finding my footing. Every day, I would jog a mile, allowing my mind to clear and find peace. Attending church and staying committed to my path of sobriety, I had reached the remarkable milestone of a year and a half clean. Lamont's call went unanswered, and I refused to let it disrupt the positive momentum I had built.

In his message, Lamont revealed that he had managed to resolve the issues with his job, ensuring that I could remain on his insurance. It was a tremendous relief to hear those words. To be honest, that was the only aspect that truly concerned me. I no longer cared about who he was with or what he was doing. I had made a conscious decision to move forward with my life and focus on my own healing. Our children were grown, and in order to find true peace, I had to detach myself from the past.

I chose not to call him back or acknowledge his message. Instead, I embraced the newfound freedom I had discovered.

On a Sunday following the sermon, the pastor extended an invitation for those seeking prayer to come forward. Despite Sasha's warning, I felt an undeniable urge to cleanse my soul and apologize to God. Overwhelmed by shame and regret, I tearfully made my way to the front of the church, where a group of twenty or more individuals had already gathered. Kayla reached out and took hold of my hand, offering comfort in her embrace. An older woman noticed my distress and guided me to a room tucked away at the back of the church. The space resembled an executive office, featuring a long table surrounded by six chairs.

In that room, the older woman inquired if I desired salvation, to which I earnestly replied, "Yes." The weight of guilt and shame was almost unbearable, causing a physical unease within me. It felt as if Sasha was vehemently opposing my decision, but I sensed that the elder saw through my facade. She firmly grasped my hands and began speaking in a language unknown to me. Although I couldn't comprehend her words, when I regained consciousness, I found myself lying on a small cot in another room.

Confusion enveloped me as I blinked my eyes open, seeking an explanation. Mother Martha, the elder woman, stood before me, accompanied by three other female elders. Overwhelmed by emotions, I immediately broke down, and Mother Mary, one of the elders, reassured me that God loved me. That day marked the beginning of my salvation journey, supported by a compassionate deacon who embodied true godliness.

The pastor encouraged new members, including myself, to attend a Bible lesson course after the church service. During one of these sessions, I encountered a kindred spirit named Ann. We instantly connected, sharing our pain and stories. The tragic loss of her parents led Ann to live with her grandmother, as no one else would shoulder the responsibility of caring for a teenage girl. Our connection grew stronger, and to this day, we exchange text messages daily.

When it was my turn to share, the pastor's gaze met mine, and he expressed disbelief. He couldn't fathom how I had managed to survive two years of consuming gasoline and carbonator cleaner without requiring an oxygen tank or succumbing to death's grasp. Astonished, he called my sister, putting her on speakerphone alongside the disbelieving deacon. They both acknowledged that my presence on this

Earth defied all odds and affirmed that I possessed a purpose—a true miracle.

Life continued to improve as I secured a job at an internet call center, eventually progressing to the position of IOP II. One day, after work, I reached a momentous decision—I had to let go of Lamont. I texted him, providing the address for resending the divorce papers. I mentioned tearing up the initial set I received while in jail. Though he read the message, no response suggested its lack of importance. I chose not to let it ruin my day and waited until after work to call him.

Lamont's call stirred no urgency, and I deliberately chose not to answer. He attempted twice, but I understood it to be inconsequential as no message was left. Once my work obligations concluded, I dialed his number. Though he appeared content, I felt indifferent and responded detachedly. Informing him about the text message regarding the divorce papers, I learned that he had indeed received it. However, Lamont confessed that things had changed, although he struggled to articulate the exact nature of this transformation. He professed his Love for me but expressed fear. Curious, I probed for clarification, and he conveyed a sense that I embodied the person he had fallen in love with, expressing his immense pride in my progress.

We began talking almost daily, yet we kept it hidden from the kids as it was still too early to reveal the rekindling of our connection. Each conversation filled me with a fluttering sensation reminiscent of the early days when we were just boyfriend and girlfriend. It had been 27 years since we first embarked on our journey together.

During our talks, I updated Lamont on the positive changes in my life. I shared with him the profound impact of finding salvation through my church and my progress at the halfway house. Lamont expressed genuine delight and satisfaction upon hearing about my newfound faith and my life's positive direction.

In turn, I asked about our children. Lamont informed me that Patricia had pursued her education and was now a successful Phlebotomist. Naheim, our other child, had secured a bank job as a call center representative. Learning of their accomplishments filled me with immense pride and joy, strengthening the bond between Lamont and me.

Two years of sobriety had transformed my life in ways I could never have imagined. My life was infused with goodness and blessings for the first time in what seemed like an eternity. The struggles of the past had shaped me, but I had emerged stronger and more resilient than ever before.

Lamont and I have been having conversations regularly for the past four months. One evening, shortly after I finished work around 9 p.m., Lamont called me seriously, expressing his need to tell me something before I heard it from someone else. My heart sank, and I couldn't fathom what it could be. We talked daily for months, and he hadn't mentioned anything significant. Lamont revealed that he had invited Shana to our house while she was in Florida, taking her daughter to Disney. I was speechless and remained silent, allowing Lamont to continue speaking. He mentioned that Shana was accompanied by her daughter and her daughter's friend and that our kids were also present.

I couldn't find the words to respond. All I could do was envision Shana—the same ex-girlfriend whom Lamont spent hours talking to every day, despite my request for him to cut off communication with her—being in MY house. I felt betrayed and foolish. Yet again, I didn't say anything, and Lamont went on to explain that they didn't even sit on the same sofa and that the kids were there, too, as if that would make the situation any better. All I managed to ask was why. Why was it so difficult for him to let go of this woman? He apologized and claimed he wanted to be honest because we were in a good place. I was heartbroken, and then I questioned him: Are you intentionally trying to hurt me?

Are you attempting to push me back into relapse? Unable to bear it any longer, I hung up the phone. I felt so numb that I couldn't cry or even get angry—I was completely detached. I didn't reach out to anyone; instead, I went to sleep.

When I woke up, I noticed messages and voicemails from Lamont, but I couldn't bring myself to read or listen to any of them. I decided not to go to work that day and took the bus to a liquor store and an auto store instead. There, I purchased a bottle of Crown Royal and a can of carbonator cleaner. I ended up drinking the entire bottle of Crown and inhaling the entire carburetor cleaner.

I reached out to Kayla and informed her of my whereabouts. The next thing I remember, I woke up at Daylight—a rehab facility associated with We Care. Daylight is where you go when you relapse. It felt as though two years of progress had gone down the drain.

"The truth will set you free, but first, it will make you miserable."

- James A. Garfield

Chapter 14

The room was cloaked in an oppressive silence, broken only by the intermittent sobs that escaped Chloe's trembling lips. It was a small, dimly lit space adorned with faded wallpaper and worn-out furniture, a reflection of the heavy weariness in the air. I stood there, my eyes filled with anger and frustration.

As Sasha's words reverberated through the air, they hit me with an unexpected force, instantly transporting me back to Daylight. I thought I had left behind. My progress over the past two years had been mercilessly flushed down the drain, leaving me vulnerable and disoriented.

The sheer intensity of the moment drowned out any semblance of coherent thought. As Chloe's sobs filled the room, the overwhelming noise made it impossible for me to hear the whispers of my mind that guided me on my path to recovery.

Frustration and anger surged through my veins, intertwining with the pain of the relapse. In a desperate attempt to regain control, to silence the chaos engulfing me, I found myself shouting at Chloe, begging her to stop. "SHUT UP, CHLOE!" The words tore out of my throat, fueled by pent-up emotions and the primal need to assert some semblance of authority over the unraveling situation.

But beneath my words' sharpness was a profound fear and disappointment. Fear of losing myself again to the dark depths of addiction and disappointment in myself for allowing Sasha's venomous words to penetrate the armor I had so painstakingly built.

As the echoes of our collective outbursts subsided, a heavy silence descended upon us. I could finally grasp the magnitude of what had just transpired in that stillness. The weight of my relapse settled upon my shoulders, a burden that threatened to crush me under its weight.

"I can't believe I was so stupid to trust him again," I muttered, the weight of my disappointment heavy in my voice.

Sasha sneered, her tone dripping with contempt. "I told you, you're so weak. You make me sick," he retorted, her words lashing like venomous arrows.

Desperation tinged my voice as I pleaded, "Sasha, please."

"Please. What?" Sasha shouted, her anger

reverberating through the room.

My mind raced, filled with self-recrimination. "Oh my God, how could I let this happen again?" I whispered, my voice a mere whisper of disbelief.

I was in Daylight for 30 days, and out of those 30 days, my deacon, Kayla, and Pastor came to visit me. I was not in the mood for prayer, but I did not want to be rude; all I did was cry... well, all Chloe did was cry; Sasha was cursing the whole time, whereas I was being dragged down the pit of confusion and humiliation.

Sasha and Chloe emerged with an unprecedented force; their presence was overwhelming and potent. It was a rare occurrence, reminiscent of a distant memory when I sought refuge in my aunt Bertha's home, a sanctuary from the storm. During those tumultuous times, Chloe introduced me to Nana, my childhood friend residing within the walls. And now, at this moment, the dynamic duo of Sasha and Chloe reawakened, relentless and unyielding.

Like a force of nature, Sasha embodied an unapologetic rebellion, a fearless spirit refusing to be contained. Her aura exuded an air of audacity, daring anyone to challenge her authority. In those moments, she became the embodiment of a true badass, embodying an indomitable spirit that could not be shaken.

On the other hand, Chloe portrayed a delicate innocence, a tender soul untouched by the world's harsh realities. Her wide eyes glistened with vulnerability, yet a quiet strength bloomed within her young spirit. Though only nine years old, she possessed a resilience far beyond her years, a beacon of hope amidst the disruption.

The three of us formed an unstoppable force, a formidable trio that defied all odds. It was as if our collective spirits fused, creating a bond transcending time and circumstance. In those moments, we stood united, a testament to the power of resilience and the unbreakable human spirit.

Chapter 15

Once again, I found myself within the confines of Daylight, a place that evoked a deep sense of embarrassment. I had hoped my time here had ended, but life had other plans. As I walked through the sterile halls, it felt like I was traversing a prison corridor, each step weighed down by the invisible gazes of judgment. But within these walls, instead of stares, a prevailing aura of compassion surrounded me, undesired and unnecessary.

Compassion was the last thing I wanted, and the mere mention of God was like salt on an open wound. I had become a pawn in the cosmic game, deceived by a higher power and Lamont. What purpose did my existence on this earth serve if not to be a mere plaything, a fool for others to exploit? In this vast expanse of a world, I felt utterly alone, abandoned to navigate the complexities of life without a guiding hand. If there truly was a God, how and why would He be so ruthless, so cruel?

I allowed Sasha to take the reins for the first time, relinquishing control to this alter ego. It was evident that Tashonda, the name I had carried, was ill-equipped to handle the challenges at hand. Thus, I let Sasha step forward, curious to see how events unfold under this new guise.

With Sasha at the helm, a transformation coursed through my veins. The once-suppressed identity surged forward, fueled by a potent mix of defiance and determination. Tashonda's fragility melted away as Sasha rose to the occasion, poised to confront the obstacles with a ferocity unbeknownst to her predecessor.

The stage was set for a new chapter, where Sasha's audacity and unyielding spirit would navigate the treacherous waters of life. It was a gamble, a leap of faith into the unknown, with uncertain consequences. Yet, at this juncture, I was willing to take the risk, to challenge the fates and carve out a destiny that external forces would not dictate.

As Sasha surged forward, propelled by a newfound sense of agency, the tale of resilience and self-discovery unfolded. The seeds of transformation were sown within the depths of Daylight, where vulnerability intertwined with strength. Within this crucible, I would discover the power of embracing my true self, unafraid to confront the world and defy the odds.

And so, with Sasha leading the way, the journey into the unknown began a journey marked by uncertainty but also brimming with the potential for profound growth and redemption.

During the group session, Sasha reveled in the opportunity to unleash her inner turmoil upon the vulnerable souls who bared their wounds. A mischievous smirk played upon Sasha's lips as she absorbed the words shared by each participant, their stories intertwining with her internal chaos.

Among the group, there stood Nate, a Caucasian man hailing from the depths of North Carolina. He mustered the courage to reveal a haunting truth, confessing that the tragic loss of his 19-year-old son rested solely on his shoulders. Nate recounted a heart-wrenching tale, recounting how he had rolled a joint laced with cocaine, unknowingly leading his son down a devastating path. It was a choice that had devastating consequences, as the grip of cardiac arrest snuffed out his son's young life. Tears streamed down Nate's face as he admitted his guilt, each drop heavy with remorse and unrelenting grief. His anguish found solace in the shattered fragments of his soul, his only respite found within the numbing embrace of drugs.

At this moment, Sasha lashed out, fueled by her pain and anger. Her voice cut through the air, dripping with bitter disdain. "Dumbass," Sasha sneered, her words piercing the room like shards of ice. "Of course, it's your fault. What kind of idiot gets his son hooked on drugs? Why didn't you just kill yourself instead of taking his life?"

Sasha stared into Nate's red, swollen eyes, filled with an intricate tapestry of hurt and fury. Not once did she blink, instead choosing to retreat from the group, retreating to the solitude of her room, shutting the door behind her. Tashonda, overwhelmed by a wave of remorse, yearned to extend an immediate apology, but Sasha, an embodiment of defiance, refused to entertain the idea. Chloe, burdened by the weight of the situation, could only weep and weep, her tears an echo of the collective pain that permeated the air.

The simmering anger that coursed through our collective being seemed on the verge of eruption, an ominous force that sent shivers down our spines. Even Sasha, whose name was Phoenix, could not escape the unsettling dread that enveloped us all.

As I sat in the confines of my room, gradually finding solace in the soothing embrace of calmness, a hunger propelled me down the hallway towards the communal eating area. A simple orange caught my attention, a respite from the storm brewing within. Yet, as I retraced my steps towards my room's sanctuary, Nate followed, his presence unexpected and unwelcome.

I turned around, prepared to wield the innocent orange as a weapon of defense, a tangible extension of my anger. His gaze fixed upon me, Nate questioned the depth of my fury, seeking to understand the source of my turmoil. At that moment, whether it was Sasha or Phoenix who responded, the words rang out sharply, "Why aren't you angry at yourself, murderer?" Without uttering another word, I retreated into my room, shutting the door with resounding finality.

The passing of days melded into weeks, signaling the impending return to We Care, a prospect I dreaded with every fiber of my being. The notion of the forthcoming walk of shame, after having made progress within the confines of Daylight, weighed heavily on my conscience. A sense of disappointment loomed over me, a shadow that whispered of perceived failure despite my earnest efforts.

Within the walls of Daylight, cell phones became artifacts of the outside world, temporarily confiscated and locked away in a place devoid of their comforting presence.

As I prepared to depart, uncertainty gripped me. Had Lamont attempted to reach out? Had his calls gone unanswered, his voice left unheard amidst the storm of my journey?

Sleep enveloped me on the eve of my departure from Daylight, weaving vivid tapestries in the realm of dreams. In this nocturnal reverie, I stood before my house, the door swinging open to reveal Shana's figure. A surge of unbridled fury consumed me, and with a shovel clutched tightly in my grasp, I unleashed a torrent of violence upon her. Dragging her lifeless form into the open, I resorted to the unthinkable, the rev of my car engine heralding an act of unspeakable brutality. Awakening in a pool of sweat, I realized with a shudder that the malevolence lurking within me had taken on a sinister form, a haunting presence that refused to dissipate.

Morning arrived, casting a pale glow upon the horizon. Then, Kyle and Jeff, the designated transporters, materialized before me, ready to accompany me back to We Care. As I approached the van, a perplexing sight unfolded. Nate, the bearer of sorrowful tales from Daylight, was also making his way toward the vehicle. A quizzical expression crossed my face, silently questioning his intentions. Kyle's voice sliced through the air, breaking the uneasy silence as he revealed the unexpected truth. "I see you've met Nate," he declared, his words laced with a hint of surprise. "He's new to We Care."

The disbelief courting through my veins found an outlet in whispered exasperation, barely audible beneath my breath. Nate brushed past me, his presence marking an unforeseen addition to our journey. The remainder of the ride to We Care passed in a solemn hush, a veil of silence draping over our thoughts. Uncertainty and unanswered questions hung in the air, mirroring the intricate complexities of our shared destinies.

Chapter 16

We finally arrived at We Care, and upon stepping into the familiar surroundings, a wave of mixed emotions washed over me. Raven, my ever-reliable roommate, awaited my return with open arms and an aura of unmatched compassion. Her nurturing spirit manifested in the meticulous arrangement of my belongings, each item meticulously placed in its rightful spot. With a heartfelt embrace, she enveloped me in a cocoon of understanding, her eyes brimming with concern and curiosity.

As we settled into the comforting familiarity of our shared space, Raven implored me to share the tumultuous tale that had led to my relapse. With unwavering support from the other members of our tight-knit crew, their eyes fixed upon me with an intensity that mirrored their genuine Care and concern, I embarked upon the arduous task of recounting the painful journey.

Words flowed from my lips, a cascade of raw honesty and vulnerability, as I delved into the depths of my experiences within the confines of Daylight. Raven, attentive and receptive, absorbed every syllable, her presence a testament to the strength of our bond.

The crew gathered around me, their voices a symphony of support and camaraderie. They lovingly referred to me as T, a testament to our bond and the strength I embodied within our tight-knit community. Their unwavering belief in my resilience reverberated through the air, serving as a resounding reminder that I was not alone in my journey.

In the sanctuary of our room, nestled within the walls of We Care, the air became charged with a palpable sense of camaraderie. Raven, a pillar of unwavering support, extended a comforting hand and offered words of solace. Together, we waded through the tangled web of emotions, embracing the vulnerability that bound us and seeking solace in the collective strength that emerged from our shared experiences.

The connection among our crew deepened within the confines of We Care, where healing took root and personal transformations blossomed. We became more than just individuals battling our demons; we became a united force, offering unwavering support and understanding as we navigated the tumultuous path to recovery.

"You are our rock, T. You've got this," Raven's voice

rang out, infused with unwavering support and belief in my ability to overcome. Her words served as a lifeline, a reminder of the strength within me.

But amidst the chorus of encouragement, there came an unwelcome discordant note. Another voice, filled with bitterness and despair, dared to defy the prevailing optimism. "Damn T, if you relapsed, then there is no hope for us," the words tumbled forth, dripping with defeatism. In an instant, my instincts kicked in, and I vehemently retorted, the fire of determination blazing in my eyes. "Don't you ever say that!" I exclaimed, my voice quivering with a mixture of frustration and defiance. It was a proclamation that held the undeniable truth of our shared humanity, our inherent fallibility.

Yet, amidst the charged atmosphere, a nasty voice laced with cruelty sneered through the cacophony. "Yeah, a human bitch," it spat, weaving a thread of disdain into the fabric of the moment. A surge of anger coursed through the rest of the crew, their voices rising in a chorus of protest and outrage directed at the source of the provocation. Confusion swept through their ranks, for Nate's presence had not yet been properly introduced. Kyle, recognizing the need for clarification, interjected, intending to shed light on the situation during our upcoming group session. However, the timing of the introduction proved to be a cruel twist of fate.

Faced with the brewing storm of animosity, I seized the opportunity to provide context, to mend the frayed threads of understanding. Addressing Nate directly, in the presence of our crew, I offered my sincerest apologies. "I am truly sorry," I said, my voice heavy with genuine remorse. "I am sorry for the loss of your son." The weight of those words hung in the air, casting a somber pall over the room as the unspoken understanding of shared pain permeated our collective consciousness.

Chapter 17

Weeks became an elusive passage of time, and the hallowed doors of the church remained untouched by my presence. Kayla had persistently urged me to return, asserting that the church was where my heart belonged. Yet, despite her fervent pleas, I declined, for it was not the company of my fellow congregants that I spurned. Rather, it was the lingering attachment to the people I had grown to love, who had become an integral part of my life.

Alas, fate had dealt me a harsh blow, plunging me back to the lonely stage of a fresh start. The contours of my life had been radically altered, and my job, once a secure foundation, crumbled beneath my feet. Unemployment engulfed me, shrouding my days in a cloak of uncertainty.

Restricted within the walls of my abode, I found solace in the virtual embrace of my companions. Bound by the confines of a Partial Hospitalization Program (PHP), I relinquished my freedom to venture beyond the premises for a grueling thirty days. Yet, strangely enough, this confinement held a peculiar charm. Within the familiar abode, we assembled, basking in the warmth of shared experiences.

Melodies would ripple through the air, intermingling with the threads of our conversations. Like ethereal whispers, words floated gracefully, weaving a tapestry of camaraderie. Together, we would immerse ourselves in the captivating world of movies, where stories unfolded like blooming flowers, evoking laughter, tears, and a profound sense of togetherness.

It was a life condensed, distilled into the essence of simplicity. Amidst the confines of our shared space, we discovered the extraordinary within the ordinary. We delved deep into the recesses of our souls, unearthing the jewels of our dreams and fears. Through these interactions, we forged bonds that transcended the physical boundaries, forming an intimate, nurtured, and embraced community.

A flicker of curiosity sparked, urging me to delve into the forbidden realm of Lamont's messages. With a hesitant yet determined resolve, I unlocked his number, prepared to immerse myself in the enigmatic world of his apologies. Four messages awaited me, each a thread of his remorse woven with delicate words.

Lamont's voice resonated through the air. Each syllable was imbued with a sincere repentance that tugged at the strings of my heart. He confessed his transgressions, confessing that his intentions had never been to inflict pain upon me. Rather, he sought to lay bare his mistakes, his desire to embark on our renewed journey with a clean slate. He bared his soul in this moment of vulnerability, yearning for forgiveness.

His words reverberated, carrying an underlying wisdom that echoed through the chambers of my mind. Lamont explained his reasoning, expressing that a profound sense of responsibility drove him to disclose his missteps. Aware of my ongoing recovery, he believed it was paramount for us to confront our challenges together within the safety net of a support system. By revealing his past transgressions now, he aimed to ensure that if I faltered and succumbed to the temptations that plagued my recovery, I would find myself in an environment where aid was readily available.

As Lamont's words lingered, a portrait of his remorse and genuine intentions painted itself upon the canvas of my consciousness. He yearned for redemption, a chance to mend what had been fractured between us. And in this confession, he revealed a profound understanding of our relationship's fragile nature and the delicate balance we were striving to restore.

Uncertainty swirled within me, entwined with the tendrils of forgiveness. Yet, despite the maelstrom of emotions, a glimmer of hope pierced through. For within his messages, Lamont's vulnerability had intermingled with a profound sense of responsibility and a belief in the power of second chances.

Deep down, I could respect the sincerity within Lamont's words, but Sasha and Phoenix, my ever-protective confidants, vehemently opposed such leniency. Their voices echoed within me, stubborn and indignant, vehemently declaring their stance: "Naw, fuck that."

Overwhelmed by conflicting thoughts, I mustered the strength to delete the messages, erasing them from my digital sanctuary. Seeking solace and guidance, I reached for the lifeline of sisterly love, dialing my sister's number.

Her voice crackled with fury, mirroring my indignation. She struggled to comprehend the depths of Lamont's actions, grappling with the audacity of bringing Shana into the sanctuary of our shared home, all while I was flourishing in my fragile state of recovery.

In the depths of my sister's anger, I found solace. Together, we navigated the tumultuous sea of emotions, clinging to each other as steadfast anchors. With each impassioned word, she reinforced the importance of self-worth and the necessity of preserving the progress I had painstakingly achieved.

Kayla faced a daunting task as she tried to guide me through the murky depths of my emotions. I had entered a new state of mind where I simply didn't care anymore. It was as if I had surrendered, throwing my hopes and dreams in the towel. Exhaustion consumed me physically and mentally, and I reached the sobering conclusion that I was fighting a battle that held no meaning. I wholeheartedly believed I was a lost cause, destined to wander through life.

Chapter 18

As I sat in the group session at We Care, my mind was consumed by a haze of numbness. After spending 30 days in Sunshine, a rehabilitation center, due to a relapse, I found myself back in the familiar surroundings of We Care. The weight of disappointment hung heavily on my shoulders as I remembered Lamont's words about having Shana in my house. It felt like two years of progress had been thrown down the drain.

Lost in my thoughts, I couldn't help but question how everything had spiraled out of control so rapidly. It was hard to distinguish whether the blame rested with Sasha or me, but the situation was nothing short of a nightmare. If this was some twisted joke God was playing on me, it certainly didn't feel funny.

During the initial weeks of my return, I sought solace in solitude. I isolated myself, trying to make sense of the chaos that had unfolded in my life. Now and then, I would catch Nate glancing in my direction. I pretended not to notice, avoiding direct eye contact, as if I could escape the tumultuous emotions that his presence stirred within me. However, an undeniable energy emanated from him that felt pure and genuine.

HOW MY ADDICTION SAVED MY LIFE

For a fleeting moment, I felt remorse for the harsh remarks I had directed at Nate. It was as if his gaze reached deep into my soul, reminding me of the interconnectedness we shared in our struggles. Perhaps he understood the pain and frustration that had driven my words, and in that brief instance, I regretted the hurt I had caused him.

The room around us was filled with a mixture of people at various stages of their recovery. The walls were adorned with motivational posters, their vibrant colors starkly contrasting the somber atmosphere that permeated the group. Some individuals wore expressions of determination, their eyes filled with hope for a better future. Others seemed worn down by their battles, their faces etched with the scars of their past.

Kyle's voice echoed through the room, urging me to snap out of my reverie. It was a gentle yet firm reminder that I needed to face the reality of my situation and confront the challenges ahead. The words lingered in the air, pulling me back to the present moment and urging me to find strength within myself.

In that room, surrounded by fellow warriors fighting their demons, I realized that We Care was not just a place of recovery but a sanctuary where broken souls sought healing and redemption. And though my journey had taken an unexpected detour, I knew deep down that I had the power to reclaim my life and rewrite my story, one day at a time.

Chapter 19

Weeks trickled by, and gradually, I found myself starting to enjoy the group sessions at We Care. I hadn't mustered the courage to return to church yet; I needed time to unravel the tangled web of confusion God seemed to have woven around me. Lamont tried reaching out, but my mind wasn't ready to hear from him. Instead, I sought solace in connecting with my sister to ensure my children were okay. As long as they were safe, it truly mattered to me in those uncertain moments.

Thankfully, Sasha and Phoenix had taken a back seat in my life for now. On the other hand, Chloe occasionally appeared, causing my emotions to unravel. Whenever this happened, I made sure to retreat to the privacy of my own space. My We Care family, however, was truly remarkable. They never judged me, and their support was unwavering. The only comment I ever heard from them was, "T, you're only human, and we've got you. We're all we've got and need to be there for each other." After hearing those words, I could only break down and cry. I sank to my knees, and as my tears flowed, the others joined me, enveloping me in their embrace. It was a powerful moment of shared vulnerability and profound understanding.

I experienced a conflicting mix of shame and relief in that raw and emotional space. I felt ashamed for being the person who had always demanded strength from others while simultaneously being unable to show the same compassion when confronted with weakness. Yet, the relief came from being surrounded by those who understood and were willing to offer solace when I needed it the most.

Amidst the tears and embraces, Kayla's entrance into the room went unnoticed by me. Only when I opened my eyes did I realize she was there, the two of us remaining on our knees. Her arms wrapped around me in a comforting bear hug, and she began to pray. Despite my feeble attempt to wiggle away, I lacked the emotional and physical strength to resist. So, I stayed on my knees, surrendering to the Lord's prayer and the words Kayla spoke on my behalf. I listened intently as she thanked God for bringing me into her life, feeling the weight of my brokenness and the uncertainty of whether God intended for Lamont and me to reconcile.

Questions swirled in my mind, wondering why so many obstacles continued to litter my path. The trust I had once held in God wavered, and attending church remained daunting. But for now, I allowed myself to find solace within the walls of We Care, seeking understanding and support from those who walked a similar journey.

As the weeks progressed, I slowly began to open up during group sessions. No longer confined to the premises, I took advantage of my newfound freedom, engaging in activities like jogging and leisurely walks. The area surrounding We Care boasted various delightful seafood restaurants and convenient grocery stores, serving as pleasant distractions from the turmoil. The money I saved while working at the call center allowed me to indulge in these small pleasures.

One particular day, I strolled toward the swing chair located at the back of the house, my book in hand. To my surprise, Nate occupied the seat, seemingly oblivious to my presence. I halted, hoping he would sense my discomfort and vacate the spot. However, Nate remained unmoved. Frustration crept within me, and I turned to leave, only for Nate to leap up from the chair and block my path. I instinctively stepped back, managing to mutter a polite excuse.

It was the first time I truly took notice of Nate's appearance. For a white guy, he wasn't bad-looking at all. Standing tall at about 6'2" and weighing around 220 pounds, he had a military-style haircut that perfectly framed his dirty blonde hair. His baby blue-grayish eyes complemented his captivating smile. The fine lines etched across his face betrayed the weariness and stress he carried. He had a rugged neatness as if he wore a perpetual five o'clock shadow.

For a brief moment, we stood there, our gazes locked. His voice pierced the silence, breaking my trance. He said softly that I was the most beautiful black woman he had ever seen. I blinked in surprise, momentarily lost for words. All I could manage was a sincere thank you before he turned and walked away. I remained rooted to the spot, caught off guard by the unexpected compliment. "Damn, he is fine," my inner voice remarked, usually belonging to Sasha. But this time, it came from deep within myself.

As I watched Nate's figure retreat, a subtle trace of his natural scent lingered in the air. It left me feeling slightly dizzy, my thoughts swirling. At that moment, I couldn't deny the stirring of attraction that had awakened within me, intertwining with the turmoil of my emotions.

Chapter 20

As Thanksgiving approached, the intensity of our group sessions heightened, magnified by the emotions surrounding the upcoming holiday. It was a bittersweet reminder of the families we were temporarily separated from. For some, the distance was bearable; for others, the weight of being apart from loved ones became unbearable, leading to tearful breakdowns.

To uplift spirits, I offered to cook Thanksgiving dinner for everyone at the house. The thought of creating a warm and comforting atmosphere, even within the confines of We Care, brought a glimmer of hope to my heart. It was an opportunity to foster a sense of family and togetherness, providing solace during this challenging time.

Deep down, I longed to reach out to Lamont, Naheim, and Patricia. The memories of our shared past weighed heavily on my mind. However, I knew healing and letting go of my anger and bitterness was essential before attempting reconciliation. It wouldn't have been fair to call them, fueled by unresolved emotions, not knowing how the children would react or if it was the right time. And so, I chose to focus on my journey toward healing, trusting that the time for communication would come when the wounds had mended.

Thanksgiving Day enveloped the house with a sense of warmth and anticipation. We gathered around the table, indulging in a feast of turkey, stuffing, gravy, cranberry sauce, candied yams, green beans with smoked turkey necks, macaroni and cheese, and a delectable sour cream pound cake. We Care generously covered the costs, reminding us that even in our darkest moments, there were still glimpses of Care and compassion.

Sitting together, talking and laughing, we forged connections that resembled a makeshift family. Nate, seemingly drawn to my presence, made a point to sit beside me. It made me slightly uneasy, though I shrugged off any concerns, not wanting to create unnecessary tension. We engaged in lively conversations, sharing our stories and finding solace in each other's company.

As assigned chores rotated among us, fate seemed to play a naughty hand. Nate and I were paired for kitchen duty, further intertwining our paths. We took turns washing dishes, and it was Nate's turn as I began sweeping the floor. I couldn't help but steal glances at him, watching him roll his sleeves past his elbows. Startled by my thoughts, I quickly averted my gaze, feeling the heat rise to my cheeks.

Intent to complete my task, I urged Nate to finish washing the dishes so that I could mop the floor. He must have noticed my distraction, for he turned and smiled at me, causing my heart to flutter. Refocusing my attention, I resumed sweeping, determined to maintain my composure. But then, unexpectedly, Nate playfully grabbed a handful of suds and flung them at my face. In a split second, my outrage exploded, and I shouted in disbelief.

"What the hell, man?!" I exclaimed, feeling a mix of irritation and surprise. Nate immediately realized the gravity of his actions, his face reflecting a mixture of regret and concern. He swiftly retrieved a paper towel and attempted to wipe away the suds from my face. At that moment, our proximity intensified, our faces mere inches apart. Snatching the paper towel from his hand, I took charge, hastily removing the suds from my face.

Once the suds were gone, Nate mentioned some in my hair. His remark made me chuckle, acknowledging the unspoken rule about not touching a black woman's hair. Laughter bridged the brief tension, forging a lighthearted connection between us. Nate graciously backed away, and I retreated to the bathroom to ensure my hair was free of lingering suds.

Looking at myself in the mirror, I couldn't help but giggle at the situation's absurdity. The suds were nowhere to be seen, and I laughed in amusement at the unexpected turn of events. Little did I know that this playful encounter would mark the beginning of a journey filled with unexpected connections and a blossoming friendship that would forever change my path to recovery.

Chapter 21

The atmosphere in the group became charged with anticipation as Kayla introduced her innovative idea for the session: the Hot Seat. I watched as a chair was placed in the center of the room, forming a circle of participants around it. The concept was simple yet powerful. The person sitting in the Hot Seat would face a barrage of questions from Kayla and the group members. It was a raw and vulnerable experience, as you had no idea what question would be directed at you.

As the session progressed, it was finally Nate's turn to take the Hot Seat. The group unleashed a torrent of questions, each more probing and emotionally charged than the last. I couldn't bring myself to make eye contact with him. A part of me wanted to shield myself from the weight of his pain, from the intensity that radiated from his eyes. I wondered why it was so difficult to meet his gaze and acknowledge the shared vulnerability we all experienced in that room.

Reluctantly, Nate answered the questions that were thrown at him. The room fell silent as he recounted the heartbreaking story of smoking marijuana with his son. He explained that it was a celebratory act to honor his son's high school graduation. Little did he know that the marijuana they smoked was laced with deadly Fentanyl. Nate's voice trembled as he revealed that it was his son's first experience with any kind of drug, rendering his young body unable to withstand the lethal combination.

As he continued to speak, Nate's anguish was palpable. Tears welled in his eyes, threatening to spill over. This was the first time he had spoken openly about the tragic events. He recounted the frantic attempts to revive his son through CPR, but it was too late. His son had passed away before the ambulance reached the hospital. The weight of guilt bore down on Nate's shoulders, a burden he would carry for the rest of his life.

Despite his immense pain and remorse, Nate expressed gratitude for the years he had shared with his son. He acknowledged the precious memories and the love that bound them together. At that moment, a profound realization washed over me. Bearing the guilt of providing the substance that took his son's life, this man still found solace in his faith. He honored God, continuing to navigate the challenging recovery journey with resilience and an unwavering spirit.

Emotions coursed through me as I reflected on Nate's story. Here I was, consumed by anger and bitterness, blaming God and denying His presence in my life. Yet, my family was still alive, while Nate had lost his beloved son. The stark contrast between our experiences struck me with a forceful realization. I had allowed my pain to blind me to the blessings surrounding me. I had failed to recognize the preciousness of life, the power of forgiveness, and the strength of faith Nate exemplified.

In that transformative moment, I felt a newfound empathy for Nate. The walls I had erected around my heart began to crumble, allowing compassion to seep in. I understood that the journey toward healing involved healing ourselves and extending understanding and forgiveness to others. Nate's story became a poignant reminder of the power of resilience, the capacity of the human spirit to find redemption even in the face of unspeakable loss.

Chapter 22

The journey of self-discovery and faith led me back to the doors of my church. Silently and without explanation, I returned, seeking solace and redemption in the familiar embrace of my pastor and deacon. They welcomed me with open arms, without judgment or interrogation. The unconditional support of my church family enveloped me, helping me comprehend the importance of God's timing and the need to trust the intricate process of life.

My church family showered me with understanding and guidance, helping me to unravel the layers of anger and bitterness that had consumed me. They reminded me that despite my rejection of God, He had never rejected me. They reassured me that God had been with me throughout my journey, even in the darkest moments, and that His love would never falter or forsake me. Slowly but surely, I began to believe those words, rekindling my faith during my recovery.

I became a regular attendee at church once again, though I hesitated to approach the altar for special prayers offered at the end of the service. The wounds within me were still healing, and I wasn't ready to fully surrender to God's will. Nevertheless, I immersed myself in the sermons and teachings, soaking up the wisdom and comfort they provided.

Alongside my spiritual journey, I resumed the practical aspects of rebuilding my life. I began filling out job applications and exploring opportunities at call centers and loan companies. The We Care staff, including Kayla, Kyle, and the rest of the We Care family, cheered me on, proud of my progress. Five months of sobriety had brought about a remarkable transformation within me, filling me with a renewed sense of purpose and strength.

During one of our group sessions, it was my turn to face the Hot Seat. Being the first to ask a question, Nate delved into the painful memories that haunted me. His question revolved around my descent into inhaling carburetor cleaner and gasoline, a destructive path I had taken. I confessed that I didn't have a definitive answer as to why I had turned to such harmful substances. Perhaps it was an escape from the pressure of being a super mom, wife, and college student. I mused that my troubled upbringing and the shadow of schizophrenia in my family might have played a role, but the root cause remained elusive.

The questions grew more personal, and when the

topic of my relationship with my children arose, tears welled up within me. The estrangement from my kids weighed heavily on my heart, and I doubted if they would ever find it in their hearts to forgive me for the pain I had inflicted on our family. Nate's compassion prompted him to rise from his seat, reaching out to offer comfort. However, Kayla intervened, signaling for him to hold back. She took over the questioning, probing into my feelings regarding Shana's involvement with Lamont. Rage surged within me, but Kayla's reminder to focus solely on my perspective dispelled the anger. I mustered the strength to admit that perhaps Lamont was better off with Shana. Kayla's voice turned stern as she asked if I wanted my family back, and my whispered " yes " response escalated into a resounding shout. Her smile illuminated the room as she encouraged me to take the necessary steps to reclaim my family, assuring me that Lamont still loved me.

As Christmas approached, the We Care house buzzed with anticipation. A Christmas tree adorned the living room, and we decorated the house together, infusing it with warmth and festive spirit. The request for me to cook once again for everyone filled me with a sense of comfort and belonging. My way of recreating the familiar traditions brought my family together.

During our preparations, Nate asked if I knew how to make Jerk Chicken. I quizzically eyed him, questioning his knowledge of such a dish. With a grin, he revealed that his foster mother, who was Jamaican, had introduced him to the flavors of his upbringing. This revelation sparked a playful banter between us. I confidently asserted that I could make Jerk Chicken, spicing it up just how he liked it. Unconsciously, a hint of flirtation laced our words, though it remained innocent and lighthearted.

As Christmas Eve arrived, the house buzzed with activity. Clad in basketball shorts and a tank top, Nate offered his help amid the bustling preparations. His physique, displaying sculpted muscles and a tattoo sleeve, caught my attention. I couldn't help but squint, attempting to discern the intricate details of his tattoos. It seemed my curiosity got the best of me, for Nate playfully flexed, teasingly remarking, "Really, dude?" Laughter filled the air as he explained that the tattoo represented a bleeding heart with thorns and an angel—a symbol of the pain he carried within his bleeding heart and the presence of his son, his angel.

Amidst the laughter and camaraderie, Nate and I engaged in a subtle dance of attraction. It was innocent, a playful exchange of words and glances that added a touch of brightness to our lives. Christmas day arrived, and we gathered around the table to feast on Mild and Spicy Jerk Chicken quarters, sweet potato casserole, collard greens with smoked pork legs, macaroni and cheese, and pineapple upside-down cake.

Amid the joyous celebration, Nate handed me a small gift bag, wishing me a Merry Christmas. Surprised, I questioned its contents, and as I unraveled the tissue paper, I discovered a pair of Bluetooth earbuds inside. I couldn't help but wonder how he knew that I wanted them. Nate simply replied that he had observed my continued use of wired earbuds and thought I might appreciate an upgrade. Grateful for the thoughtful gesture, I thanked him sincerely.

Then, in front of everyone, Nate asked if he could have a Christmas hug. The room fell silent as all eyes turned to us, their expressions filled with knowing smiles. Unsettled by the attention, I attempted to maintain a distance, but he pulled me closer. The embrace felt innocent, yet it sparked an electric current within me. Time seemed to stand still as I became acutely aware of his presence—the way he felt, the intoxicating scent that enveloped him. I silently prayed for the moment to end, for him to release me. Eventually, we pulled apart, and the room erupted with joyful smiles. The sudden attention made me blush, and in a lighthearted attempt to dispel the awkwardness, I jokingly told everyone to "shut up." Oddly enough, no one uttered a word, allowing the moment to pass in silence.

Chapter 23

The comforting embrace of my church community continued to draw me closer to the altar with each passing Sunday. The pull to seek God's forgiveness and guidance grew stronger within me. After attending a particularly uplifting service, I decided to run to clear my mind and let my thoughts settle. Swiftly changing into biker shorts and a crop top, I equipped myself with my new wireless earbuds. However, just as I was about to immerse myself in music, a half-naked Nate emerged from the shower, clad only in a towel wrapped around his waist. Startled, I mutter, "Get thee behind me, Satan!" before hastily darting out the door. Lost in my thoughts about Nate, I realized I hadn't even played any music; instead, I found myself engaged in a conversation with myself about the unexpected sight. I scolded myself for allowing such thoughts to distract me, pleading for divine intervention to overcome my momentary weakness.

Later that night, I sought solace in self-gratification, indulging in an intimate moment of release multiple times. I couldn't help but think that I might need new batteries for my pleasure. The following morning, I received an unexpected phone call from America Loans, notifying me of an interview opportunity. Excitement coursed through me as I shared the news with everyone at We Care. Their genuine happiness for me and their high-fives reinforced my belief that I was finally getting back on track. I expressed my gratitude to God for this chance.

Shortly after, my phone rang again, with my daughter Patricia on the other end. Although uncertain about answering the call, fearing potential rejection, I mustered the courage to pick up. She asked if I could attend her birthday party at Universal Studios next month. Overwhelmed with joy, I eagerly accepted her invitation and thanked her before hanging up. The prospect of reuniting with my daughter awakened a renewed sense of purpose.

The following Sunday, I went down to the altar during the church service, ready to pour my heart in prayer. The phone call from my daughter stirred something profound within me, prompting me to seek forgiveness from God. Tears streamed down my face as I fervently apologized to Him for my previous actions and implored His guidance and strength. The weight of my remorse and the enthusiasm of my pleas filled the sacred space. I repeatedly whispered, "I am so sorry," and pleaded with God not to let me falter or sabotage my progress.

To my delight, everyone at We Care expressed their happiness for me upon learning about the job opportunity. Surprisingly, my focus was not on Lamont during this time. My mind was set on moving forward and rebuilding my life, inch by inch.

The day of my interview with America Loans arrived, and I was meticulously dressed in my blue suit, white blouse, and black heels. Clutching my neatly typed resume in a manila folder, I was prepared to face the interview panel. Kyle accompanied me, offering his unwavering support and assuring me of my abilities. Deep down, I wanted to believe him, but the familiar self-doubt threatened to overshadow my confidence. Inner voices bickered within me—Sasha and Tashonda—yet distinguishing between them had become increasingly challenging. As we entered the America Loans office, I reminded myself that I had faced interviews before and that this was just another opportunity.

After waiting in the lobby with four other candidates, I was eventually called into an office where an oval table sat, surrounded by five individuals. Unfazed, I confidently greeted everyone with a cheerful "Good morning." To my surprise, I was offered the job on the spot. All that remained was the paperwork for a background check and other formalities. The only concern raised was the need for a car since the position required me to travel to various America Loan Companies as a Lead Auditor. I explained that I didn't own a car, but I assured them I would save up and purchase one within the given 90 days. Kyle's words of encouragement echoed in my mind as I realized he had always been right.

My first day at work was scheduled for two weeks later. My ease with numbers impressed my colleagues, and they inquired about my car. Though I had saved up three paychecks, every dealership I visited required a co-signer despite my good credit. Frustration threatened to dampen my spirits until we encountered a dealership where a beautiful 2014 Smokey Grey Dodge Dart caught my eye. Admiring the car's sleek appearance and rims, I knew it was the one. However, I was sinking when the salesmen asked for insurance information. I had forgotten about that crucial detail. Panicking, I had no choice but to call the one person I had hoped to avoid—Lamont.

After what felt like an eternity of hesitation, Lamont answered the call. I explained my situation, mentioning the car purchase and the need for insurance. With unwavering kindness, he readily provided me with the necessary details, congratulating me on my new car and assuring me that I could reach out to him anytime. Grateful for his help, I relished owning my vehicle. The salesmen handed me the keys, and I felt indescribable independence and accomplishment. This was my first significant purchase made entirely on my own. As I drove back to the We Care house, I beeped the horn, and suddenly, a crowd of around 15 people emerged, radiating happiness and excitement. With my new car, we no longer had to rely on the We Care van for transportation, and the newfound freedom filled us all with joy. I expressed my gratitude for their support and offered to help whenever possible.

As the day unfolded, I couldn't help but feel a mixture of gratitude and satisfaction. Lamont had come through for me, and I acknowledged his assistance. However, it was clear in my mind that his involvement ended there. The car symbolized my newfound independence and the beginning of a stable future.

Chapter 24

As I embarked on the two-and-a-half-hour journey back to what used to be my home, a mix of nervousness and anticipation coursed through my veins. It had been two and a half years since I last set foot there, and I had no idea what to expect from my children. Surprisingly, I felt neither concern nor worry about seeing Lamont again. My focus was solely on reconnecting with my children.

As I pulled up to the familiar house, I noticed that the once towering oak tree in front of it was no longer there—a silent reminder of the many arguments I had with Lamont, urging him to have it removed. Stepping out of the car, I rang the doorbell, and Lamont greeted me. My eyes locked onto him, taking in his appearance. He looked tired, as if he hadn't slept in days, but he was undeniably attracted.

His long dreadlocks cascaded over his broad shoulders, and he wore a tank top accentuating his physique. He moved aside to allow me to enter, and as I stepped inside, memories flooded my mind. I couldn't help but wonder where that woman had sat when she was in my house. My gaze quickly scanned the surroundings, searching for something, although I couldn't quite grasp it. Lamont asked if he could hug me, and I agreed without hesitation. As our bodies pressed against each other, I felt myself melting at that moment. Despite all the pain and resentment, I still loved that man deeply.

He was the only one I could imagine being with, yet I also wanted to hate him. Breaking away from his strong embrace, I inquired about the whereabouts of everyone else. Lamont informed me that Patricia and her friends were on the back patio while Naheim was in his room. I made my way to Naheim's room. First, my heart still harbored bitterness towards him for involving the police and obtaining the injunction against me. Technically, I shouldn't have been in the house, as the injunction was indefinite—those were Naheim's words in court. Naheim's door was open, and I descended a few steps into his room.

He had his back turned to me, engrossed in his music production, surrounded by multiple monitors. "Hello," I said, breaking the silence. He turned around, his face lighting up as he replied, "Well, hello there. How are you?" "I'm good. How about you?" I asked. Anaheim responded, "I'm good too. You look good." I thanked him and left his room, making my way to the back patio where Patricia and her friends were gathered. The moment I opened the double doors, blasting music hit my ears, and Patricia rushed towards me, enveloping me in a tight hug. It was an emotional moment, and I fought back tears, feeling the weight of all the time lost. After a while, I sat on the patio, ensuring not to overstay my welcome. Lamont sat in the living room, engrossed in a Kung Fu movie.

It was a pastime we used to enjoy together, and for a while, we sat in silence, surrounded by a comfortable familiarity. Eventually, he broke the silence by mentioning how good I looked. I thanked him, and he responded, "I don't bite." I replied, "I know," and he suggested putting my luggage in our room. Unsure of how to respond, I hesitated for a moment before agreeing. Lamont picked up my bags and headed down the hall, leaving me to grapple with my swirling thoughts. Doubts and insecurities threatened to cloud my mind, and I wondered if she had been in that room.

I quickly shook off those thoughts and focused on the present. Lamont reassured me later that she had only been in the living room. As I glanced around the house, I observed its cleanliness—although the dishes were clean, they had been left in the sink, a minor annoyance. The pool area, on the other hand, was well-maintained. Overall, it seemed the best effort had been made. Despite my reservations, I decided to sleep in our shared bedroom. Once again, we became husband and wife, and how he made love to me felt like an apology. It wasn't about him; it was all about me, and I couldn't deny that it was wonderful.

The following morning, we awoke early and enjoyed a day filled with family fun at Universal Studios. Patricia and I fearlessly embarked on the craziest and scariest rides while Lamont and Naheim contented themselves with capturing the memories through photographs and indulging in amusement park treats. It was a bustling and joyful day, but exhaustion had settled deep within me by the end. We bid farewell to Universal Studios around 6 p.m., returning to the house for cake and presents. I presented Patricia with a gold heart pendant from Kay Jewelry Store, and her joy was palpable as she enveloped me in a warm hug. Knowing that I had to leave the next day, Sunday, and with everyone else having worked on Monday, we cherished our last moments together.

Although I expected to feel regret after being intimate with Lamont, surprisingly, I didn't. Instead, a sense of contentment settled over me. Perhaps it was because Lamont had been a part of my life since we were high school juniors, or perhaps it was because he was the father of my children—the love I felt for him ran deep. The next day, my phone rang as I drove back to West Palm Beach. It was Lamont; without preamble, he professed his love for me. He acknowledged that he had always loved me and sincerely apologized for all the pain he had caused.

In turn, I apologized for the hurt I had inflicted upon him. It was a cathartic conversation, and I felt a sense of relief as if a weight had been lifted off my shoulders. I genuinely meant every word of my apology and sincerely regretted all the pain I had caused. I told Lamont it would be best to remain friends and allow nature to take its course. I believed God was preparing us for the next chapter in our lives, and we needed to let Him work His miracles. From a spiritual family, Lamont was hurt but understood and agreed with my sentiment. I explained that I should not be alive— God had a purpose and plan for me.

With an "I love you" exchange between us, we ended the call, but our conversations continued for several months. Each day felt like we were dating anew, and I couldn't help but feel butterflies whenever he called. It was like we were rediscovering each other, navigating a brand-new relationship. Amidst this, I offered to send money to help Lamont, but he insisted that I shouldn't worry about it and that he was proud of me. I began diligently saving my money, harboring a secret plan to secure an apartment in West Palm Beach.

No one else knew about it. Realizing I needed to trust God's process rather than forging my path, I prayed fervently for healing. Starting with my relationship with Naheim, I asked God to bring peace to my heart, even if I couldn't comprehend the reasons behind certain events. I pleaded for His guidance and acceptance of His process, relinquishing my need to understand and allowing Him to work in His own time. I recognized that the relapses I had experienced were meant to strengthen me, although the significance had eluded me then. God wanted me to trust Him, and although it took time, I was slowly learning to do just that.

Chapter 25

Lamont surprised me with a visit to West Palm Beach. As we spoke on the phone, I found out he was driving, and he asked me what I was doing. Without thinking twice, I replied, "On the swing, where I usually am." Unbeknownst to me, Nate was nearby. Since my return, he had been a constant presence, and I noticed a change in me. I couldn't deny it—I felt different. Suddenly, Lamont mentioned the presence of a large mango tree in front of the house. It took a moment for his words to sink in, but as soon as they did, I leaped off the swing and power-walked to the front of the house. And there he was—Lamont—looking like he stepped straight out of a GQ magazine. His dreadlocks were pulled back into a ponytail that cascaded down to the middle of his back.

He wore a blue and white basketball set with white Nikes, and I couldn't help but admire his appearance. Introducing him to the crew, I noticed that Nate was nowhere to be found. Lamont and I decided to take a walk in a nearby park. It felt surreal—like a first date—despite having spent over 30 years together. My hands trembled, and butterflies fluttered in my stomach. Why was I so nervous? We had a deep conversation as we strolled, Lamont promising not to hurt me again. He admitted that he didn't know what he was doing, acknowledging his mistakes in bringing Shana into our marriage and home. He assured me that he had severed all ties with her, and even when she was at the house, it never felt right. Our children agreed—it didn't feel right.

I explained to him that it was never meant to feel right. How could it, with another woman intruding into our sacred space? I had begged God to help me forgive her, not for her sake, but for my own. Now, looking back, I felt sorry for her. Once I let go of my anger and accepted that I needed to take responsibility for myself—not blame Sasha, Chloe, or Phoenix—things began to change. It was a bitter pill to swallow, but I realized that the excuses I had created were just excuses. They were born out of a young girl's insecurities, a part of me that I had integrated into my identity.

Lamont and I went to a restaurant to grab something, and I couldn't help feeling self-conscious about eating in front of him. I took small bites when he wasn't looking, my nerves getting the best of me. Lamont was in town for the weekend and rented a hotel room. He asked if I would stay with him, and my heart wanted to say no, but ultimately, I agreed. His eyes mirrored the one he had given me 30 years ago when I said, "I do." The next few months blended into a year, and Lamont and I spoke daily—during our lunch breaks, on my way home, and before we went to bed. It became a routine, a comforting thread woven into the fabric of our lives. Suddenly, my plans to stay in West Palm Beach began to shift. But as time passed, I noticed Nate's behavior towards me change. He seemed distant and acted as if I had done something wrong.

Fed up with his attitude, I confronted him, asking his problem. At first, he insisted there was nothing, but I knew he was lying. Finally, he confessed, saying, "Okay, you want the truth? Your husband is playing you again. And for a smart woman, you act dumb about him." Nate observed that I was doing well, having remained clean for a year. He pointed out that I was best when Lamont wasn't around. Damn, he was right. A small voice whispered in my ear, urging me not to let any man tear me apart.

Chapter 26

As the days turned into months, Lamont and I thrived in our renewed friendship, reminiscent of how we first met over 30 years ago. Initially, I didn't like him much; he exuded arrogance, but eventually, his charm and bad boy persona grew on me. Our conversations were open and honest, and I confided in him about my plans to find an apartment.

Lamont seemed understanding, though perhaps a little hesitant, asking if I was sure about my decision. I expressed my fears of rushing into anything and my determination not to let anyone, not even him, lead me back to a relapse. Lamont nodded, acknowledging my concerns. Life at We Care Housing continued to improve, and I was even asked to speak and become a sponsor—a humbling and honorable role in helping others recover from addiction. God had indeed worked in mysterious ways.

Reflecting on my journey, I realized that my addiction had inadvertently saved my life. I had hit rock bottom, and in my darkest hour, I found my faith, my true connection with God. This transformation was not an easy climb; it had its share of bumps, bruises, and stitches, but I learned to climb, maintain, pray, and worship. Each step up the mountain was a testament to God's grace and love. One day, it dawned on me that it was time to return to my family.

I had received apartment offers, but something didn't feel right. Then it hit me—I needed to return to where I belonged. God had placed me at a job requiring me to get a car, which was the final piece of the puzzle. I knew it was time to return to my loved ones. I hesitated before sharing the news with Kayla, fearing her reaction. She cared deeply for me and worried about my well-being. Despite her initial reservations, she understood my decision and promised to support me.

My We Care group meeting announcement stirred mixed emotions among the residents. They were both happy and sad to see me leave. Kayla surprised me with a little party, and I received heartfelt gift cards and a Certificate of Completion of the Program. As I shared my decision with my church family, my testimony flowed freely, touching the hearts of those present. They wept, shouted praises, and celebrated my transformation. I felt humbled and grateful for the love and support they showed me. I gave my job a two-week notice, declining their offer of more money. My family was my priority, and no amount of money could sway my decision.

God had a plan for me, and I trusted everything would fall into place. The last day arrived, and I left the We Care community with sadness and hope. The overwhelming love and encouragement from everyone gave me the strength to move forward. The morning of my departure, my car was already packed. As I dressed, I couldn't help but feel a mix of emotions—sadness, nerves, excitement—but I pushed aside the negative vibes and silently worshiped God.

I walked through the house one last time, bidding farewell to the place that had been my refuge for months. It was heart-wrenching to leave this newfound family, but I knew it was time to reunite with my own. As I left, I offered comforting words to my friends at We Care Housing, assuring them that this was not a goodbye but a promise to keep in touch. The journey back home was emotional, but deep down, I knew I was following God's plan.

Chapter 27

As I settled back home, I wasted no time seeking employment. I was determined not to burden anyone, including my family. Within a week, I received a phone call from a pharmaceutical company offering me an interview for a Lead CPhT position (Certified Pharmacy Technician). Miraculously, I got the job and started within a week.

It was evident that God had orchestrated it all; I just had to trust and believe in His plan. Looking back, I realized God's timing was impeccable, and He knew what was best for me. Working in a pharmaceutical company, I made more money than ever before, and remarkably, I could do it from the comfort of my home. I was in awe of God's power and ability to provide beyond my wildest dreams.

It was like God was showing off, and I couldn't help but laugh at the thought. This job was not just about financial gain; it allowed me to be a supportive partner to Lamont in ways I never could before. With God's strength flowing through me, I could lift him during his challenging times, something I could never do in the past. My newfound strength came from relying on God's power rather than my own, and it was a refreshing and freeing feeling. It became evident that God's presence in our lives made us a formidable force capable of overcoming any challenge. However, I soon learned that the enemy wasn't happy with our transformation.

It fought back, trying to undermine us at every turn. But God's protection and love shielded us, and we emerged victorious each time. I shared my experiences and faith with my children, emphasizing the power of prayer and the importance of giving thanks in good and bad times. My daughter, Patricia, had prayed for my return and witnessed the power of her prayers being answered. I encouraged her to continue seeking God for everything and never underestimate the power of prayer.

My son, Naheim, was more skeptical, questioning why bad things happen if there is a God. I explained that it's okay to seek understanding from God when faced with difficult questions. I shared with him how God had turned our lives around, and deep down, I sensed he was starting to grasp the concept. I didn't pressure him but instead urged him to continue praying for our family and seeking God's guidance. As we continued our journey together, I knew God's plan for our lives was far greater than we could ever comprehend. He had taken us through the darkest times to bring us to the brightest days, and I was forever grateful for His love and grace.

As we grow in faith and understanding, I believe that God will continue to lead us on the path of righteousness, and together, we'll overcome any obstacle that comes our way. The journey ahead may not be without challenges, but with God by our side, we are ready to face whatever comes our way.

Chapter 28

As my life fell into a more balanced rhythm, I saw the beautiful transformation in my relationship with my children. It wasn't an instant fix and required patience and understanding, especially with my son, Naheim. I knew that forcing anything would only push him away, so I let things unfold naturally, allowing time and love to heal any lingering wounds. We took it slow, one step at a time, and I ensured that God remained at the center of our lives.

I now understand the importance of prioritizing family and work life while maintaining an unwavering devotion to prayer. Planning and organizing have become essential aspects of my routine, though I admit it's not always easy. There are days when I am utterly exhausted, and finding the words for prayer is difficult. I silently reach out to God in those moments, knowing He hears even my unspoken cries. There have been occasions when I've drifted off to sleep while praying, feeling comforted by the knowledge that God's love and protection surround me.

Despite the challenges and rough days that inevitably arise, I have not entertained the idea of relapse, not even once. The power of God's presence in my life is evident, and I am grateful for His grace that sustains me. I praise God for leading me out of darkness and into a life filled with love, hope, and purpose.

My family has become a testament to God's incredible healing power, and it's heartwarming to see the positive changes that have taken place. Our bond has strengthened, and I cherish every moment we spend together, knowing that it is a gift from God. As we continue to navigate life's challenges, I am confident that with God's guidance, we will conquer any obstacles that come our way. My children have grown to understand the significance of prayer and the faith that keeps us anchored, and I am overjoyed to see them embrace their spiritual journey.

Life is far from perfect, and we still have ups and downs, but the difference now is that we face them together, with God at the helm. I am in awe of the blessings that have come our way and the strength God has instilled in me. Each day is a new opportunity to grow in faith, and I know that as long as we keep God first, everything will fall into place. I trust in His divine plan for our lives and am grateful for the immense joy and peace He has brought into our hearts.

This journey has taught me that anything is possible with God's love and grace. I can't help but praise God for the miraculous transformation that has taken place within my family and myself. His wisdom guides every step we take, and I am eager to see what other wonders He has in store for us as we continue to walk hand in hand with Him. The road ahead may have twists and turns, but with God as our constant companion, I know we will overcome and thrive in His abundant love.

Chapter 29

It has been five fulfilling years since I returned home, and my heart is brimming with gratitude for the beautiful life that God has blessed me with. My connection with We Care has not waned, though the pain of losing four dear friends to drug overdoses weighs heavily on my heart. I pray fervently for their families, seeking solace and strength during this difficult time. God has taught me the value of empathy and compassion, and I use my journey to encourage those struggling.

As time passed, my focus shifted to another challenge that struck close to home—my son Naheim's skin issues. Witnessing his distress over the scars on his face motivated me to seek a solution. Nurse Shyla, a kind soul at my workplace, came to our rescue with Activated Charcoal Soap. The positive results inspired me to purchase more soap from her, but she saw potential in me that I couldn't envision. She encouraged me to make soap and start my own business, but I hesitated, unsure if I had the time or expertise. However, with the unwavering support of Lamont, Shyla, and my children, I mustered the courage to embark on this new venture.

Soapmaking became my therapeutic escape, a

delightful blend of creativity and science. Despite the initial challenges and failures, I was dedicated, knowing that my family stood firmly behind me. Lamont's reassuring words reminded me that the first year was a learning experience and that setbacks were inevitable in any new endeavor.

Research became my constant companion, and I immersed myself in soapmaking, devouring every piece of knowledge available. I studied videos, took notes, and honed my skills, treating them with the same enthusiasm as preparing for a crucial exam. My determination and perseverance paid off, as after a year and a half of trial and error, I finally crafted the perfect organic soap. These soaps catered to people with sensitive skin, and their hypoallergenic properties made them suitable for all.

The journey of building my business, Naturalessence2021 LLC, was both rewarding and challenging. Making soaps became an act of self-care, infusing joy and relaxation into my life. I relished fulfilling custom requests from people with specific skin needs. With God's guidance and blessings, our soap line expanded to include various products, from oils and sugar scrubs to bath bombs and body butter.

While I anticipated a surge of support from my

family due to our reconciliation and my sobriety, the reality was quite different. The lukewarm response from my non-immediate family was disheartening, and I wrestled with hurt and disappointment. Nevertheless, I realized that life is unpredictable, and not everyone will react as expected. I leaned on God's grace to navigate this challenge, learning to appreciate genuine support from unexpected sources.

Through it all, God reminded me to remain steadfast and not to allow setbacks to define me. Much like a baseball game, life throws curveballs our way, and the key is to let them pass without losing our sense of purpose and determination. God's plan for me and my family has been filled with triumphs and trials, and I continue to trust in His guidance as I embrace the journey ahead.

My heart overflows with thanksgiving for the lessons learned and the love that surrounds me. I remain grateful for the opportunities God has placed in my path, including my business, which is a testament to His grace and my determination. Every soap I make carries a piece of my story, a reminder of the power of faith and the miracles that can unfold when we trust in God's plan. As I take each step forward, I know God is walking beside me, guiding me with love and unwavering support.

Chapter 30

Reflecting on my journey and the transformations God has brought into my life, I am filled with an overwhelming desire to help others find their path to healing. I have become a mentor for both young and elderly addicts, offering them the guidance and support they need on their road to recovery. I find that addicts tend to open up more when they connect with someone who has experienced similar struggles and triumphs. Sharing my story with them, holding nothing back, allows them to see the raw and unfiltered reality of addiction and redemption.

I stress the importance of believing in a higher power with every person I mentor. The journey to recovery is challenging enough, but navigating it alone can feel insurmountable. Through my own experiences, I have realized that surrendering to a higher power is the key to finding strength and hope in the darkest moments. I passionately share with them how God has been a driving force in my life, guiding me and my family through our trials and tribulations.

I openly talk about the ups and downs, the highs and lows of my journey, leaving no detail untold. I want those I mentor to understand that God's plan is vast and intricate, and the obstacles we face may be stepping stones toward a greater purpose. My testimony serves as a reminder that God's grace and mercy never falter, even when we turn our backs on Him. It is a testament to His unwavering love and faithfulness.

As I mentor these individuals, I feel a profound responsibility to share my experiences with as many people as possible. I promised God I would use my story to inspire and encourage others. Every trial and challenge I have overcome has molded me into who I am today—a living testament to God's transformative power. I let them know that it is okay to be vulnerable, to expose their weaknesses, and to embrace their journey with all its imperfections.

I want those I mentor to understand that God has a unique plan for us, and we may not always comprehend the reasons behind our experiences. But through faith and trust, we can find solace in knowing that God is walking alongside us, guiding us every step of the way. Even in my moments of weakness and stubbornness, God never abandoned me. His love remained constant, offering forgiveness and redemption.

The reward of mentoring lies in witnessing the progress of those I guide and seeing them embrace the power of God's love and their spiritual journey. I am grateful for the opportunity to be a source of hope and inspiration for those who are struggling, and I will continue to share my story, for it is a testament to the miracles that can happen when we surrender our lives to God's grace.

Epilogue

The author wholeheartedly attributes her success and transformation to her unwavering faith in God and His divine help. She firmly believes that her life's journey, from the depths of addiction to redemption and healing, was guided by a higher power. Throughout her narrative, she emphasizes that she takes no credit for the positive outcomes in her life but rather gives all the praise and glory to God.

The author's testimony is a powerful example of how surrendering to God's plan and trusting His guidance can lead to profound personal growth and blessings. She acknowledges that her addiction, which once seemed like a curse, became a blessing in disguise because it brought her closer to God and helped her discover her purpose.

Through her new series, Chronicles of Denise, the author delves into the different facets of her personality, represented by the alter egos Tashonda, Sasha, Chloe, and Phoenix. These characters symbolize her struggles and complexities on her journey, allowing readers to relate to life's various challenges.

In sharing her story and promoting her new series, the author's main goal is to provide hope and inspiration to others. She hopes that her book will be a source of support for families dealing with addiction and other hardships. The author's optimism about the series stems from its candid portrayal of real-life issues, such as schizophrenia, alter egos and family imperfections. She aims to shed light on the importance of understanding and compassion in dealing with such struggles.

Overall, the author's journey from addiction to redemption and her dedication to sharing her story in Chronicles of Denise exemplifies her strong faith in God's grace and the transformative power of His love.

Chronicles of Denise

In "Chronicles of Denise," the author takes readers on a compelling journey back to her childhood, offering a deep insight into her life and experiences. The series explores her challenges as an only biological child, including physical and emotional abuse, sexual assault, homelessness, abandonment, and a drug-infested environment. Additionally, the narrative delves into the impact of having a mother with schizophrenia, enduring bullying, and encountering racism.

Through "The Chronicles of Denise," the author aims to convey hope and resilience. One of the central themes is the importance of recognizing and embracing God's love, which the author herself discovered after hitting rock bottom. She hopes her readers will understand that they don't need to reach such depths to realize God's love for them. The series serves as a reminder that healing and redemption are possible, even in the face of immense adversity.

Looking to the future, the author intends to continue writing and educating others. Her future works may touch on self-care and explore roller-coaster events, likely involving the alter egos Sasha, Phoenix, and Chloe. These characters represent different aspects of her personality and experiences, providing a unique perspective on her journey.

As the author navigates her personal life, she remains committed to spreading awareness and inspiring others through her writing. While her alter egos, particularly Phoenix, have demonstrated challenging characteristics, the author acknowledges that their complexity mirrors the complexities of life itself. The future holds further exploration of these facets, and her dedication to helping others remains a focal point of her writing career.

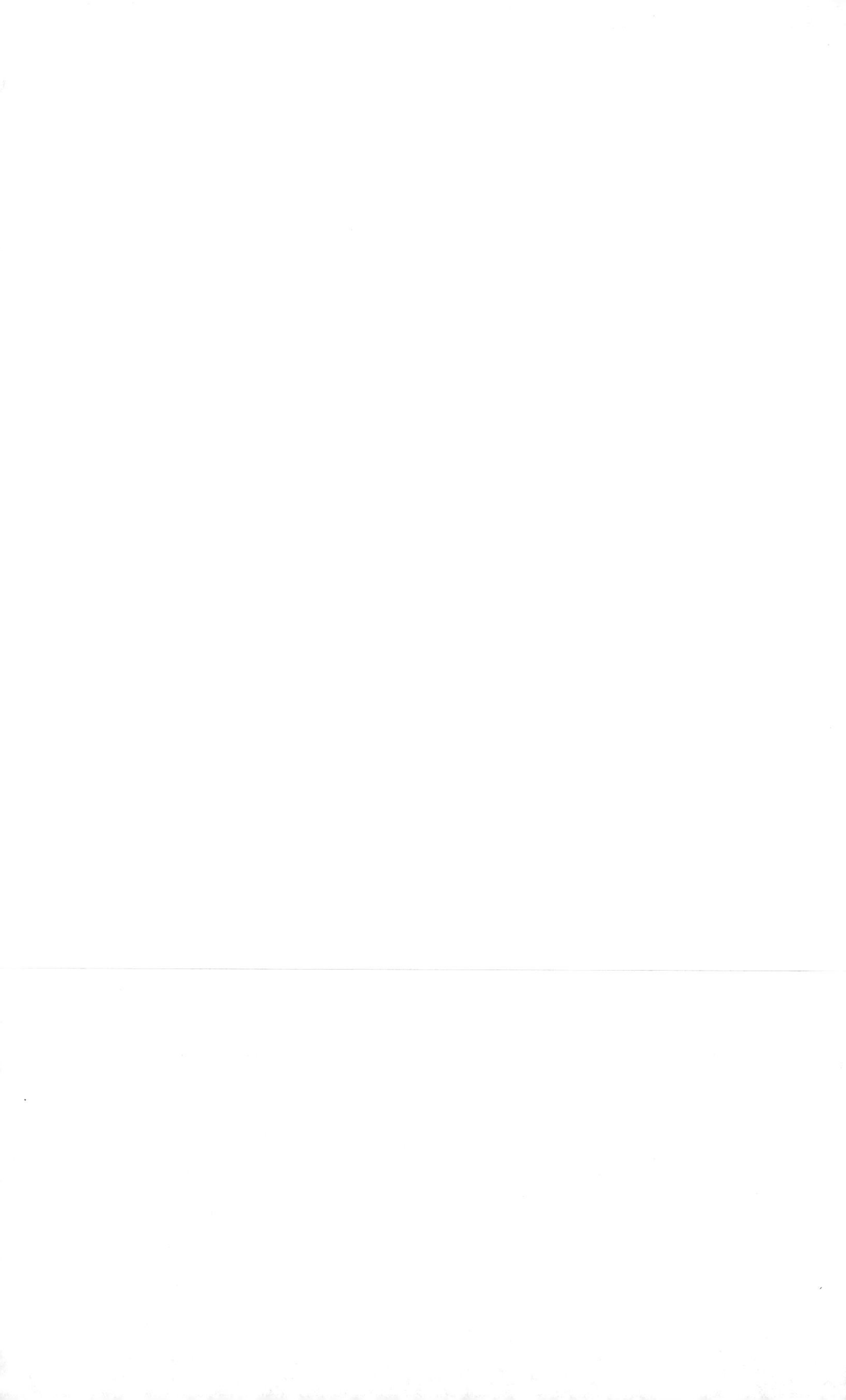